—CAMPHILL VILLAGES—

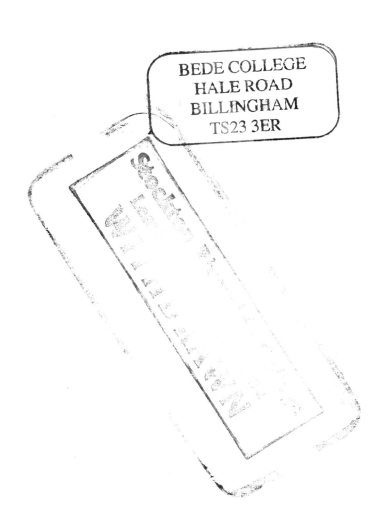

SECOND EDITION 1988

PUBLISHED BY CAMPHILL PRESS
ON BEHALF OF
THE CAMPHILL VILLAGE TRUST

© CAMPHILL PRESS 1988

FIRST EDITION 1977

BRITISH LIBRARY CATALOGUING IN PUBLICATION DATA

1. WEIHS, ANKE   2. TALLO, JOAN   3. FARRANTS, WAIN
CAMPHILL VILLAGES–SECOND EDITION
1. MENTALLY HANDICAPPED PERSONS. COMMUNITY CARE

ISBN 0-904145-29-8

EDITORS: ANKE WEIHS AND JOAN TALLO
REVISED EDITION EDITED BY WAIN FARRANTS

PHOTOGRAPHS BY MEMBERS OF CAMPHILL COMMUNITIES,
PETER MERNAGH AND MICHAEL PEART

PHOTOGRAPH OF RUDOLF STEINER BY KIND PERMISSION
OF VERLAG AM GOETHEANUM

DESIGNED AND TYPESET BY HOUGHTON KIRBY

PRINTED BY WYNSTONES PRESS. GLOUCESTER.

CAMPHILL VILLAGES

EDITED BY ANKE WEIHS & JOAN TALLÓ

——REVISED EDITION——
EDITED BY WAIN FARRANTS

BEDE COLLEGE

* 0 0 0 0 1 0 5 9 *

— CAMPHILL PRESS —

—CONTENTS—

Painting by Eric Steadman (Botton)

—INTRODUCTION—

—THE FOUNDING OF CAMPHILL—

The Camphill Village Communities sprang from the Camphill Rudolf Steiner Schools for Children in Need of Special Care, founded in 1940 in Scotland by Dr. Karl König (1902-1966) of Vienna, who came to Britain from his native Austria as a refugee from Nazi oppression.

Karl König was a follower of Dr. Rudolf Steiner (1861-1925), the Austrian teacher, philosopher and seer, who introduced new meaning and new methods into agriculture, remedial education and many other branches of therapeutic, social and cultural activity. Karl König, himself a physician, had had years of experience with children with special needs prior to coming to Britain.

From the original small estate – Camphill – acquired near Aberdeen by Karl König and his young staff in 1940, an international movement has developed which, to begin with, comprised a number of residential schools for children with special needs. From the outset, these schools were run as integrated communities in which children and staff live together in smaller or larger households.

Camphill Schools for Children in Need of Special Care are private, non-profit-making, charitable institutions to which relevant Authorities in the different countries refer children for care, treatment and education until they are of school-leaving age.

—THE START OF 'VILLAGE COMMUNITIES'—

In 1954, a group of parents in Britain approached Karl König with the question as to what could be done for their children with special needs when they reached school-leaving age and adulthood. Hospitals, occupational therapy and training centres were dotted about the country as alternatives to remaining at home, but opportunities for people with special needs to make meaningful contributions, economically as well as socially, within their local environments or elsewhere were rare.

The need of the parents and their growing, maturing children with special needs coincided with an inherent Camphill ideal to establish village communities in which men and women, with special needs or otherwise, would work together and create new forms of social and cultural life. The original group of parents rose to the challenge and with faith, perseverance and few funds, set out in search of a property suitable for a first village community of the nature envisaged by Karl König and his friends in Camphill.

An estate which had belonged to W. F. Macmillan, one of the very first parents and benefactors of Camphill, was found and purchased and in September 1955 at Botton Hall, the Camphill Movement embarked on a new venture – the venture of the Camphill Village Communities. Botton Village became the model for the many other village communities throughout the Camphill Movement, both in Britain and abroad which, in turn, have inspired others outside the Camphill Movement to find new ways of living for and with people with special needs.

In this booklet, we should like to share some of the ideals of the Village movement, and we shall tell a little of the story of the Botton village community itself, with reference to the communities which have followed it.

Dr. Karl König

—A NEW SOCIAL ATTEMPT—

An editorial abridged from 'The Cresset'. *Michaelmas 1956.*

For many, the ideals and principles of the Village Community may seem remote and unworldly. Yet we know of no one who has been to Botton village who has not been gripped by the immediacy of the social attempt being made there. The moment you enter the dale, you know you have entered a new province; its newness is already inscribed into the atmosphere, it casts a spell on you – not the spell of the cloister, the retreat, but the spell of the future. The future blows like a fresh wind down the dale and you love the feel of it in your face.

There is some talk of a revival of the middle classes in this country and it is fairly clear that a moral or spiritual revival is meant, not a political or economic one. A much-appreciated gentleman of the press produced some profound ideas a few weeks ago. He expressed concern at the spiritual decadence of human society in this country and foresaw a social and economic catastrophe after which a revival within the middle classes would take place – resulting in a repopulation of the foresaken and barren

Teacher and children harvesting potatoes (Botton).

Joseph carrying tray in Camphill Coffee Shop (Malton)

dales and glens of the country, giving rise to a new culture based on values of moderation, with work as a matter of ethics and responsibility and not as an economic commodity.

His was a poignant utopia emerging out of the rubble of a fragmented society – not by virtue of any powerful leadership, but by virtue of impoverishment and naked human values.

Does the term 'middle class' now perhaps mean that there is a growing number of people who are beginning to realise that social salvation does not lie in extremes, that it lies neither in the ideologies of the East or the West, nor in this or that party or creed, that a goal cannot be reached by falling prey to Scylla or Charybdis on the way?

The resources of the earth are gigantic and mankind has taken them for granted as unquestioned conditions of existence to which there was no thinkable limit. But in recent decades, the results of man's insatiable use of the elements have begun to loom threateningly all over the world. Earth – how many hundreds of erstwhile fertile acres slip away yearly, almost irretrievably eroded by chemical over-treatment! Water – read of the empty reservoirs, receding ground water, polluted rivers and lakes, oil-encrusted oceans! Air – good air has become a precious thing – smog can be had anywhere, and from another aspect, our air is controlled by traffic regulations and in some parts its 'highways' are over-congested.

And who can measure those resources of moral health and creativeness which must sustain the conditions man is forging for himself, but which are equally imperilled? We are all impoverished in our joy, in our love, in our essential freedom to be whole and human.

Thus, the new Village situated in a remote Yorkshire dale might be one of those places the gentleman cited meant, for it was not born out of affluence, nor are there great resources of knowledge and experience to draw on, for the venture is too new and wisdom will have to be gathered on the way. But our hopes and the hopes of many others are pinned upon it. May it carry on in strength and clarity of purpose.

Julia, ex-Botton villager, now at Camphill Devon.

——THE THREE GREAT ERRORS——

—A CHAPTER IN COMMUNITY LIVING —

From an address delivered by Dr. Karl König at the Official Opening of the Botton Village Community, 27th May 1956. Abridged.

It is now more than ten years ago since the idea of a Village Community for adults with special needs and others first sprang up in the hearts of those who work in Camphill, but in the pursuit of other necessary tasks the idea lay dormant.

Two years ago, in February 1954, I addressed a gathering of parents about a village community in which young men and women with special needs would have a vital place, and it seemed as though the idea had gained in strength and impetus during the years of silence, and now here we are in Botton with many friends and well-wishers, and it is as though we were called upon to christen the child that quickened here nine months ago. I had a deep desire to offer a spiritual gift to this newborn work, and when I meditated on the matter I began to consider the trends of modern civilization during the last two hundred years. I discerned three milestones along the way modern mankind has been going which, to my mind, have a bearing on what we want to do here.

'AGNOSTICISM'

At the beginning of the last century, a certain idea struck root in the minds of men. It sprang out of the period of Enlightenment which flourished mainly in France during the middle of the 18th century. In that period, rational thinking was acknowledged as the only means of solving the riddles of existence. Men like Voltaire, Diderot, Rousseau, d'Alembert and others tried to break with the faiths of the different religious creeds.

The ideas which evolved out of the rationalism of this period and which spread very quickly amongst men set forth that, until then, people had held that man was created by God, but in reality man had created God. He had done so in order to satisfy a yearning for the supersensible. Man's power of fantasy had first invented the gods and goddesses of ancient times and later, when his thinking prevailed over his fantasy, he conceived the idea of the one God as Prime Mover of all existence. But the Age of

11

Rock climbing outside Glencraig.

Enlightenment had made men clever enough to see that there was no divine Prime Mover at all.

Other ideas developed out of this one and led to the wave of agnosticism prevalent in the 19th century. A great variety of scientific misconceptions sprang up, as a result of which man suddenly found himself in a position of being master of the earth. He began to harness Nature with the reins of modern technology and the increasing success of his inventions strengthened his conviction that he was indeed master of the earth.

The destructive forces of atomic energy, the insane striving to reach other planets, are an outcome of a first fundamental error which began to beset the minds of men just 200 years ago.

'SURVIVAL OF THE FITTEST'

In the course of the last century, another error was added to the first. It arose in the field of natural philosophy. Some of the great discoveries in palaeontology had made it increasingly obvious that man as an organism is part and parcel of Nature. The similarity of his bodily structure with that of the higher animals had become apparent. Equally apparent was the similarity between some of the higher and lower animals and the fossils of earlier times. In the minds of learned men like Lamark, Geoffrey de St.

Hilaire, Goethe and others, the idea was kindled that all animals have a common origin and gradually developed from lower to more differentiated forms. The animal kingdom was like a tree; the branches and twigs were the many different classes and species of animal. The idea of Evolution was born.

It was a most satisfying idea because the tremendous variety and diversity of animals could now be grasped by means of one all-embracing formula. Likewise, no divine power had created man in his own image; the abundance of life had developed out of mud, as it were, in the course of millions of years with man as the peak of evolution, from whence he could look back with awe and pride.

Darwin's book on *The Origin of Species* was published in 1859. In it the idea of evolution was given a further interpretation with the author demonstrating that 'natural selection' was the key to all development. The driving force in evolution was the 'struggle for existence'. When he propounded these fateful ideas, Darwin was little aware of how they were to influence the minds of men for coming generations. Where Darwin started, Hitler and Stalin continued. The idea that the coming about of a world of living creatures was due to nothing but the lower instincts and the 'survival of the fittest' was the second great error that has clouded the minds of men in our time.

'MEASURABLE INTELLIGENCE'

The third error can be found in the field of psychology and had a long, long tale of deception. At the end of the last century, the idea of 'intelligence' became a psychological theory. Galton (a cousin of Darwin), in his 'Anthropomorphic Laboratory', was one of the first to classify and grade the types of humans according to their intelligence. The German psychologist and anthropologist, W. Wundt, continued to develop the idea of measurable intelligence and Binet, the Frenchman, devised the means to measure it. In combined effort, British, German and French psychologists raised the banner of 'measurable intelligence'.

They and others set out to demonstrate that the differences in human beings were due to the varying degrees of intelligence they possessed. By means of highly sophisticated tests and mathematical formulae, individuals were investigated and issued with intelligence charts.

These ideas permeated the entire field of education. Children were now 'scientifically' graded in different intelligence-groups, according to the amount of 'g' and 's' factors stuffed into their brains. Here lie the seeds of our managerial society.

THE LONGING FOR COMMUNITY

These are the *three great errors* which have contributed to the wars and disasters of our present civilization:

Man considers himself the master and heir to the earth and the universe, the idea of God being but a mirage in the minds of primitive peoples –

The basic instincts and the 'struggle for existence' which result in 'the survival of the fittest' are regarded as the prime mover in human development and have become axiomatic –

Measurable intelligence became the criterion according to which a man's standing in society, politics, economics, etc. is evaluated –

To deny that all this constitutes a powerful force in our modern way of life would be shutting our eyes to reality. However, other powers are also at work and although they are perhaps far less obvious, their strength is of great importance. These powers originate in the hearts of many who sense the oncoming disasters of this century with increasing certainty, and in the longing of the modern human soul for a new way of community living, a longing to meet the other person essentially and to unite with him in work and life.

The desire for new community experience is an outstanding symptom of our time. It began to appear after the end of the First World War, when young and old everywhere gathered up their worldly and spiritual resources to 'start a new life'; collective farms, schools, communities for peace and friendship sprang up.

Many of these experiments broke down, but others followed and especially in Britain the move to community had become very pronounced before the Second World War. There were, for instance, the Iona Community, and the beginnings of the Taena Community, The 'Brudherhof', the 'Barnhouse', 'St. Hilda-in-the-Fields', 'The Brotherhood of the Way' and other communities were founded. The Camphill Community, too, came into being at this time. In all these attempts there was a longing to relate to the fountainhead of all existence. 'Back to the land' became a catchword among people who left the cities to take up work on the land. Organic farming was *en vogue* and the 'Soil Association' in this country took its first steps as an appreciable body.

After the Second World War, a new factor in community-living arose. Sociologists discovered that workmen in factories and mines and the like needed a human approach. Patients in mental hospitals all at once seemed to become significant within the system, and the movement of 'Human

14

Relations' began with considerable drive and success.

Everywhere, people were longing for something which ordinary life no longer gave them, because man lives – as T. S. Eliot says:

> '...dispersed on ribbon roads,
> And no man knows or cares who is his neighbour
> Unless his neighbour makes too much disturbance.
> But all dash to and fro in motor cars,
> Familiar with the roads and settled nowhere.'

Eliot goes on:

> 'What life have you if you have not life together?
> There is no life that is not in community,
> And no community not lived in praise of God.'

In this last verse, lies the essence of all modern longing for community. Wounded existentially, men yearn for mutual help and healing. The individual wants to shed his crooked belief in the supremacy of intelligence; he wants to meet his fellows not as intelligent beings but as human ones. He desires contact with the *heart* of the other, with his eternal Self.

He also wants to regard the other, and to be regarded by the other, as something more than the sum total of basic drives and instincts. He wants to experience in his neighbour an Image of God and to confess it. And when his neighbour experiences an Image of God in him, both rise to their innate human dignity.

Finally, men need to rediscover the evidence of Divinity in the world. But a man cannot achieve this entirely on his own. In companionship with others he can regain his certainty of the revelations of God and develop strength and courage in life.

Wherever true communities are formed, the three great errors that have beset men in modern times will gradually be dispelled and redeemed.

THREE TASKS OF THE VILLAGE

Here we find the spiritual origin of our Village. It is one among other experiments in community-living. It is special inasmuch as it has set itself a special task. It wants to create a life for those unable to find a place in the outside competitive world. This could, however, be a passive task and even if carried out with the best of intentions would result in another asylum, another retreat, another place of escape, were it not for a further active factor.

The Camphill Village could be a vital experiment for future social needs. Men and women whose intelligence is, according to test standards, supposed to be inferior, will live and work with others of 'normal' intelligence, but will not regard this as a barrier between them, for it is an illusory barrier. Every human being is endowed with the same intelligence; it is the talent given to each of us when we are born. The spark can be clouded or paralysed, existentially frustrated, imprisoned in a damaged body, yet it is just here where all men are *equal*. To acknowledge this will help the 'normal' to overcome their pride, for it is pride which divides mankind into the clever and the stupid, the primitive and the advanced, the higher and the lower of his kind.

A second task is to experience that man's origin does not lie in the natural alone, but that it lies equally in the transcendent. This needs daily practice in which we shall continuously have to contend with our own weaknesses and unbelief. We shall be confronted with daily disappointment and despair. Others will not live up to our expectations and we ourselves shall soon lose heart and faith. We shall then have to be mindful of the divine seed in every human being, a seed powerful enough to overcome all difficulties and trials – if not today, then tomorrow; if not tomorrow, then later, ultimately. Here, there is a solemn *fraternity* among all men. We are brothers because we originate in the Divine and the Divine is at the same time our human potential and the incentive in our human development.

Finally, we must learn that all our work and efforts are in vain if not sustained by a sense of divine meaning. Common work, common worship, common deed and common joy, common sorrow, and commonly experienced grace, gradually create the certainty of a Divine Presence, which is a community experience of the rarest wonder.

When we succeed in kindling our enthusiasm and our love for the work we do every day, whether it is baking bread, making shoes, milking cows, we shall gain *freedom*, for true freedom can only be experienced when we devote our labours in love to a Higher Meaning.

Thus in a community can *three great ideals* of modern mankind be realized: Liberty, Equality and Fraternity – ideals that were trampled into dust and blood in the French Revolution, and which are waiting to be raised anew into the society of men.

These three great ideals, when brought forward into vital social living, will counteract and heal the effects of the three great errors. The Camphill Village is an active endeavour to contribute to this task. The outcasts of today are the forerunners of the future!

——An Appreciation—— Of The Village Community

Dr. Thomas J. Weihs. 'The Cresset'. *Michaelmas 1956. Abridged.*

It was some years back that I was taken by a forester through the woods of a large estate. We walked among the straight and even trunks of a plantation of red firs. Every tree was alike, the ground was slippery and springy from the layers of needles – no beast was to be seen, no other tree or plant, no undergrowth. Felling was easy, as all the trees matured at the same time; but the forester pointed out a slight swelling at the base of the trunks of most of the trees and, where felling had begun, it was noticed that many trunks were rotten from within.

Having shown me this diseased monoculture, the forester took me to his experiment in forest healing. In a neglected part of mixed forest he had felled small clearings around a few sound, mature trees, not aiming for any economic return, but aiming for health in the forest. We entered into an ocean of quivering green. From the grass-covered ground to the highest

After the Volleyball Match (Triform).

treetops, leaves and needles of all shapes and hues filled the space. The air resounded with the song of birds, and game tracks led through the thicket of seedlings and undergrowth. Here, uniformity and sameness were replaced by manifoldness and variety. Here was health and life. The tiniest flowers and grasses, together with the mighty, mature oaks and larches, struck a balance that made for constant rejuvenation and wholeness.

Ours is a time in which men try to live as though we were all the same. We tend to hide our diversities, our individual uniqueness, behind the artificial 'monoculture' of normality, and among the identical stems of our social monoculture, seedlings and bushes and beautiful young trees are driven into the shadow of 'abnormality'.

Jim's father is a headmaster, his three brothers gained scholarships in universities, but Jim himself is only 4 feet 8 inches (142 cm.) in height. He has not managed in school, he is spiteful and difficult. Maurice is tall and blond and handsome, but his speech is explosive, he is shy and withdrawn, given to erratic behaviour and sudden aggressive outbursts. Both his parents are doctors, his brother and sister are doing well ... Peter is a big, strong lad, but his IQ is below 50, so he cannot live among the normal 'trees' ... Doreen is a Down's syndrome, she loves everybody, but that does not fit at all ...

The Botton village community is an attempt to lend diversity of such human make-up, which our monoculture so readily discards as subnormal, to the harmony and manifoldness of community life.

The village community takes people who, in the community at large, would be classified as 'mentally defective'. This term should be understood. Most lay-people as well as doctors, psychologists and social workers are unaware of the meaning of the term 'mental deficiency'. People are inclined to take it as a medical or psychological diagnosis, which would imply an evaluation or classification of a person's condition or ability on a scientific or cognitive basis. Yet from this point of view, 'mental deficiency' has no definable meaning. It is valid only as a legal concept, ascertaining a person's peculiar position in society according to the relative danger society presents to him or he to society.

The Mental Deficiency Act provides for four categories:

Those who are unable to guard themselves from common dangers –
Those who cannot manage themselves and their affairs –
Those who, though less handicapped than the foregoing, require care and protection for their own sake –
And those requiring care and protection for the sake of others.

These are the four defined degrees of mental defectiveness which itself is defined in a supplementary clause as 'a condition of arrested or incomplete development of mind...whether arising from inherent causes or induced by disease or injury'.

Neither medicine nor psychology knows what a complete development of mind is, and we are, moreover, uncertain as to what we really mean with 'mind'. Probably in connection with the Act, people are inclined to connect 'mind' with intelligence. Yet the range of intelligence in a great majority of mental defectives is the same as that of other people. 'Mind', no doubt, includes qualities such as moral powers, but here too, the range compared to normal people proves to be similar.

Nevertheless, the wording of the Mental Deficiency Act has some positive openings. One is that 'mental defect' is an incomplete development of the mind, which means a restriction in the unfolding of personality and its possibilities of self-expression. But this implies that primarily, the mind or personality of a defective *is of the same nature*, the same make, as ours.

The other positive factor is the realisation that 'mental deficiency' is not a diagnosis of an individual condition, but is a term descriptive of a social phenomenon, that is, the phenomenon of relationship between the community and the individual.

Here is contained a challenge: to find new forms of community-living which will accept the individual, integral personality in such a way that the developmental 'otherness' becomes **variety** instead of **abnormality**, that diversity rather than uniformity becomes the foundation of healthy social life.

Thus one might say that the Camphill Village Community is an attempt to rejuvenate and heal sick forests of our time.

——CAMPHILL VILLAGE TRUST—— COMMUNITIES IN GREAT BRITAIN

BOTTON VILLAGE COMMUNITY

When you search for Botton Village along the steep and winding roads over the Yorkshire Moors, somewhere between the little villages of Danby and Castleton you suddenly come across a road-sign saying: Botton – to your great relief, because the dale is not easy to find.

THE ORIGIN AND GROWTH OF BOTTON

When, in the summer of 1955, Botton Hall was taken possession of for the new Village venture, it was a somewhat remote estate consisting of a large manor house, three farms with stables and outhouses, and three cottages, all built of local stone, which in sombre weather appears a little forbidding. On either side of the estate, the moorland rises up to a fair height with typical upland grazing and wide expanses of heather. Trees were sparse and somewhat battered by the inclemencies of the Yorkshire climate. The estate lay towards the head of the dale, where life almost seemed to have petered out. Towards the lower and outward end, there were a few more scattered farms and a parish church.

Electricity was generated for the manor house, but the farm houses and cottages had neither electricity nor sanitation. Access to the houses on the estate was along exceedingly muddy tracks and mud, in-and-out-of-doors, was a dominant feature of the early days. All in all, Botton Hall was a bleak, silent, even forsaken place and, with its rough climate and rudimentary amenities, almost a discouraging place, until on occasions, the sun came through and invested the dale with breath-taking beauty.

This must have been a reflection of the experience of the first group of co-workers and people with special needs who entered Botton to begin life there in September 1955; living in and getting to grips with this place was a formidable task for the small group of eighteen people, but the Village ideal was like an inner sun that fired everyone with that steadfastness, faith and strength which have, through the years, brought about the miracle in this Yorkshire dale.

Gradually, bathrooms were put in, kitchens renovated, heating installed – drainage, electricity, telephones – a long list of major

20

requirements, which was completed laboriously, because there were hardly any funds to draw on.

Then, one by one, the workshops were erected. Some of the initial workshops were fairly makeshift; later they were improved or replaced by new ones. The dwellings, too, underwent alterations, at first within the given structure, then with the help of the Camphill architect, they were added to, rebuilt, and in the case of one of the more angular farmhouses, which practically burnt to the ground, newly erected. Together with this, oft-times magical, transformation of the existing houses over the years, came the many new houses, warehouse, store and the like. Tree-belts were planted, paths were laid from house to house, and a system of roads built right round the whole estate.

Further land was acquired in the course of time; in 1968, a farm, with the lovely name of Honey Bee Nest, brought Botton to the head of the dale; another farm, Rodger House, purchased in the late 1960s extended it further in the other direction; and with the purchase of Nook House Farm in 1985 and Stormy Hall in 1987 Botton now includes the western as well as the eastern slope of the South end of the dale.

An important moment in the development of Botton came in 1967 with the opening of the village Community Centre in the heart of the estate.

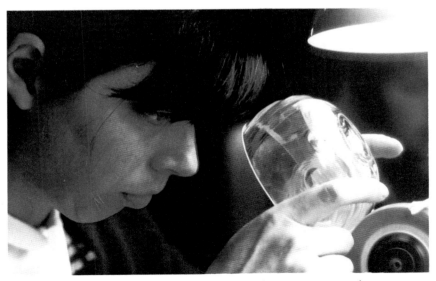

Marilyn (ex-Botton, now at Stourbridge) concentrates on glass engraving.

21

It contains a hall and stage as well as a living unit. Later a chapel was added.

Today, when you look down on to the dale from the road that runs along the moorland ridge to the city of York, you see a thriving little settlement of 610 acres, with a population of over 300 people, surrounded by carefully cultivated fields and woodlands.

LIVING TOGETHER IN BOTTON

The small group of co-workers and young men and women with special needs who first went to Botton came from Camphill Schools, either in Scotland or in England. In the context of educational establishments, the co-workers were used to educating, and those with special needs to *being educated*. One of the first lessons both groups had to learn in the new situation was to alter their attitudes towards one another. Co-workers had to learn that when people with special needs grow up, they too are *adults*, with all their obsessions, oddities, deficiencies and streaks of genius which are, when one comes to think of it, extensions of one's own oddities and deficiencies. Co-workers had to learn not to live *for* those with special needs, but to live *with* them.

The men and women with special needs in the pioneer group at Botton had to learn to realise that they were no longer going to be 'looked after', but were going to have to take responsibility, not only for themselves, but for the community. This first group has meanwhile become middle-aged and it is moving to experience their maturity and community-wisdom.

Karl König was firm in his endeavour to establish completely different human attitudes in the villages from those cultivated towards the children in the Schools and gave several leading lecture courses which have formed the basis for the self-discipline of all those who work and live in the villages.

One manifestation of this 'village discipline' was the breaking down of any distinction between 'staff' and 'patient' and the creating of an utterly mutual relationship. This, in its own terms, has required as much labour as has been expended on the physical framework of Botton. All too readily do the 'three great errors' spoken about by Karl König determine one's attitudes; things are done more efficiently and more speedily if one need not take into consideration the varying abilities and speeds of those with special needs, but sometimes people with special needs have extraordinary abilities and remarkable speeds that far exceed one's own. Equally, all kinds of issues can be discussed with far more grasp by people who are normal, yet the generosity of nature, the power of commitment to ideals, the capacity of forgiveness in those with special needs can be disconcerting, to

22

*Marvie and Kate
gathering dried
flowers (Botton).*

say the least. In the end, living with people with special needs is living with *people* and this is a symphonic task in which, at any time, any instrument can soar upwards and lead the melody to the accompaniment of all the other instruments in the orchestra.

In the early days of the village community, it seemed natural that school-leavers from the Camphill Schools and other schools for children in need of special care would progress directly from school to village. This assumption was corrected by experience. Many school-leavers, going directly into a village context, felt deprived of life-experience in the outside world and were also, because of their relative immaturity, not in a position to fall into adult life in a working community. It has become a condition of entry into a village that a young person, having left school, spend at least two, if not more, years at home, in hospital, at a training-centre, or even adrift, in order to gain as much experience as possible, including disillusionment and disappointment, before making the decision to go to a village. For a person with special needs to make this decision himself, is important. There are, of course, always some for whom the decision must be made, but these would be people in whom can be sensed a basic ability to participate in a dynamic social community.

The minimum age for entry into a village community is twenty, although under some circumstances this rule is relaxed. After his or her

Botton Doll Shop

interview with the Medical Advisor to the Camphill Village Trust, almost all people with special needs have a two-to-three-week trial visit, during which a person can experience if the village context complies with his needs and expectations and the community can take stock of what it has to offer the newcomer. By and large, there are two criteria for entry – a person should be able to work under the conditions stipulated by the Manpower Services Commission's Sheltered Workshop Scheme, and must be a potentially positive member of the social community. These criteria would seem to restrict candidates for village life. In actual fact, they allow for a surprising range of ability and disability in the villages, where there are people with very low IQs to people who may be only mildly eccentric, with blind, deaf, autistic, people with Down's syndrome, those suffering from convulsive disorders and many others.

The villages have not proved so suitable for people with psychiatric trouble (although mental handicap, even Down's syndrome, does not preclude psychiatric breakdowns), nor are they so suitable for people who are morally handicapped, in the sense of delinquency. Both these groups are inclined to be egocentric, and living with adults with special needs tends to be mutually unproductive.

Another thing assumed in the early days was that the village would offer a permanent home and work to men and women with special needs, but this has undergone considerable modification. For many people with special needs, permanence is a boon; for others it can mean stagnation. If someone feels he is being 'held' in a village community against his urge to be outside, not only is he himself frustrated, but the village is put in the false position of being some kind of restrictive provision.

Therefore, there are always some people with special needs who are encouraged to pursue their wish to find open employment. Others may be helped to acquire new outlooks by going to another village community, even abroad. There are those whose preference for hospital life, or life at home, must be recognised and respected. There are the very many for whom the village community has become 'home' in the full sense of the word. In the population of the villages, there are elements of permanence, semi-permanence and transience, in the co-worker population as well.

There are instances when mutual trust and relationship between an individual and the community break down, or when the problems of an individual impose too great a strain on the community as a whole. Although terms like 'admission to' or 'discharge from' are inappropriate to a village, a parting of ways does at times become necessary.

Botton Woodwork Shop

25

A person who has problems or who presents problems to others is often in a position to know what is needful and, if he is not articulate, there must be those who can help him to express himself. Personal talks, personal guidance and personal relationships are essential to the healthy life of everyone in a village community.

The population of the village community consists of the men and women with special needs, the youngest of whom will be about twenty, with an ageing group at the other end. It will consist of permanent co-workers, some of whom are younger and some who are likewise ageing. There will be a considerable group of young co-workers who come for shorter or longer periods, either to help in the work or to train in a particular area of community life. Then there will be a large group of co-workers' children, ranging from infancy to adolescence, not to mention those who return in adulthood to take up work in the village.

There are no 'staff' quarters and 'residents' quarters in the villages. Each household has its own mixed community, sometimes with a nucleus of a natural family. There are no dormitories; two to three people with special needs may wish to share a room – others have single rooms. These households are not 'care units'; many a visitor to a Camphill village is at a loss to know who is caring for whom!

Botton Village having grown so large, has divided into 'neighbourhoods' which has helped to decentralise the inevitable amount of organisation necessary in such a community. The neighbourhoods provide a forum for considerations of social and inter-personal contact, of money matters relevant to the households in the respective neighbourhood, and many other problems and potentials more constructively dealt with among neighbours.

The differentiation into single households and into neighbourhoods within the totality of the village helps individuals not to experience themselves as just a number in an amorphous mass but keeps alive individual incentive and initiative. It allows, in addition, for a great variety of differentiated relationships.

In the epic of life in a village community, the question of marriage among those with special needs is bound to arise. Marriage is neither 'forbidden' nor 'allowed'; it is in each case primarily a matter of responsibility, both on the part of the two people concerned, as well as on the part of the community in which they live. There have been some marriages and children, with a range of problems and casualty as well as success. These are again situations which must be handled personally and in depth. People with handicaps often have great insight into their own limitations and, although they might wish to marry, they voice hesitation in having children, not for reasons of genetics, but for reasons of not being able to include a child's existence in their relationship with one another. In such cases, necessary measures will be opened up to them.

Sex is not one of the problems of the village communities and, unless artificially induced, not a specific problem of those with special needs. In a society in which money and sex are believed to be ends in themselves, there are still people who uphold that human beings are not there to be governed by their sexual urges, but that sexual urges are components to be governed by the human being. A human being becomes the freer, the more he is able constructively to accept the circumstances in life which seem to be his – whether married or celibate, whether with special needs or normal. Fundamentally, he holds the key to his development and fulfilment as a person in his own hands, and inasmuch as people with special needs are *people*, they are as open to these things as anyone.

The care of their own person is an attribute of maturity. Some people with special needs have it to a high degree; in others it is insufficient. Much thought has been given as to how to meet problems of personal hygiene in a

Riding (Botton)

Botton Weavery

way compatible with the dignity of the individual adult in a village. Some time ago, the Health Centre was set up in the heart of the village, to which people can go to have nails and hair trimmed, feet looked after, weight taken, general condition checked and the like. This was a most popular innovation and is fully taken advantage of. There is no resident doctor in Botton. The services of the local GP are relied upon.

Still about people – because of their peculiar economic system, co-workers in Camphill centres forego pensions, and their lives are not insured. There is no retiring age. They age within the community, either remaining active or requiring withdrawal and care; what they have to give as people is important and highly valued. The same applies to ageing people with special needs.

A WORKING DAY IN BOTTON

The visitor who spends a day or two at Botton Village may well begin to feel embarrassed if not given a job to do, for Botton is a busy and diligent place. When work begins at 9.00 am and 2.00 pm, there is a surge of coming and

28

going all over Botton – people going to their work places, cheerfully greeting friends as they go by – also when work ends at 12.15 pm and 5.30 pm.

Let us take the workshops first: In the early days, the workshops at Botton were based almost entirely on the idea of crafts, and highly skilled operations were deemed too complicated for men and women with special needs. This has changed. There are, for instance, the wood workshop, with intricate machinery; the glass-engraving workshop, where exceedingly fine skill is required and achieved, and which has made quite a name for itself; and the doll workshop, with a variety of complicated operations and machining. All of these workshops have become production centres with a large output.

Weaving and candle-making are perhaps still pure crafts, but experience has shown that there must be as many types of work in a place like Botton as possible, if full employment is to be offered to people with so many diverse gifts and abilities.

All the articles made by the craft shops and workshops are of high standard. Several have been included in the British Design Centre Index, and all are sold on the open market. It was a fundamental issue for Botton that repetitive contract work should not be undertaken and that all the workshops, although run with division of labour, should allow for work of an artistic and creative nature.

Another area of work is partly associated with the workshops. In 1971, a warehouse was built to store finished products from all the villages in Great Britain and Ireland, and to relieve the workshops of packaging, marketing and despatch. Such a Central Sales Department, with all its ramifications, is a vital bridge between the workshops and the world, and requires exacting work.

Camphill Press developed out of a small graphic arts department. Since the acquisition of the first printing machine in 1973 a great deal of development has taken place here where not only the major stationery requirements for the Camphill Village Trust and its Centres, but also increasingly, books and leaflets both for Camphill and other organisations, can be designed, typeset, printed and distributed.

Botton Village being many miles away from any major shopping centre, opened a village store where foodstuffs, cleaning materials, haberdashery and a variety of household necessities can be had. Stocking, selling, accounting on behalf of a large, lively community, are sizeable tasks, ably handled by the storekeepers.

Then there is the Gift Shop, which stocks a selection of village products, including articles made in the other Camphill villages in Britain and abroad, largely for the many visitors who come to Botton at all times of the year.

The Botton Bookshop, started in 1972, has a very wide range of books to meet the interests of everyone at Botton, its many visitors and its mail order customers.

The Botton Village community has its own Post Office with a beautiful red post box in the centre of the village, and last but not least there is the manning of the central telephone system in relays around the clock. For years this has been in the hands of capable people with special needs and is a taxing task, for the number of telephone calls in and out of Botton is prodigious.

Very different is the area of the work on the land. Botton keeps a herd of mainly Ayrshire/Shorthorn cattle. The entire village has been provided with its own milk for years and milk production has increased to supply the Creamery built in 1973, where the yoghurt and Botton cheeses are made, which are sold to the general public.

The Meat Store butchers and freezes cows, pigs and sheep from Botton which have been slaughtered locally. Meat raised on organically, bio-dynamically cultivated land is particularly tender in texture and taste. The Food Centre, which started in 1973, has facilities for producing and storing jams, juices, peanut butter and many other foods, as well as freezing surplus from the vegetable gardens and fields.

Haymaking at Botton

In 1975 the old Bakery was re-established in new premises and at Martinmas 1983 it was further expanded, providing mainly wholemeal bread to the large community in Botton and to many shops in the region.

Constant tree-planting and forestry are carried on in Botton in connection with the care of the whole estate. At Michaelmas 1979 a sawmill was opened to provide the important link between the forestry, the woodworkshop and local farmers.

To be a farm worker is not as simple as it may look. The steady, reliable routine characteristic of a workshop is only in part to be experienced on a farm. There are the daily imponderables – the weather conditions, calving, lambing, and all the operations required to reap any kind of harvest in the autumn. All this demands commitment, strength, endurance and ingenuity and those people with special needs who have learned to work responsibly on the farms have, indeed, achieved a great deal.

Finally, there is the background, totally 'unproductive' yet all-important area of cooking, housework and laundry. Here again, more skill and ingenuity are required than one at first thinks, and like farming, housework is by no means merely simple routine labour suited to the less able. It is an area exposed to constant minor emergencies needing foresight as well as an ability to cope and to organise, and the area most intimately bound up with the general well-being of all in a community. Farming and cooking are also the two areas of life not confined to an eight-hour working day; they are indeed parental in the unceasing service they render to a community.

A house for people who are old, sick or need convalescence was opened in June 1985 and named Thomas Weihs House after the late Dr. Weihs, medical consultant for the Camphill Schools and the Camphill Village Trust. There the pace is a little more leisurely than in most houses but still everyone who can, participates in the house work as well as the social life of the village.

There is an activity in the Botton village community which is not one in which those with special needs are directly involved, although it has, in a sense, provided the condition for this activity, and this is the Botton Village School. This little Rudolf Steiner School, founded in 1960, has been the village school not only for the co-worker children at Botton up to the age of thirteen or fourteen, but also children from outside who come in each day by mini-bus.

A form of artistic and therapeutic movement called Eurythmy, practised in Camphill communities as well as in Rudolf Steiner Schools,

31

requires a training of at least four years and a curative eurythmist must do further training before he can practise in conjunction with a doctor. Botton village houses the third and fourth years of the Ringwood-Botton Eurythmy School. Anyone has an opportunity to do eurythmy if he so wishes. Full performances often grace the stage.

SOCIAL AND CULTURAL LIFE IN BOTTON

If the working day at Botton is intense and busy, so also is the social and cultural life of the village community. As in any true village, there is a great sense of occasion at Botton, especially when things are done on a grand village scale.

The central place the Sacraments of the Christian Community take in the life of the village is described elsewhere. This does not mean that anyone is forced to participate in the Sunday Services. Some go to the local church, four miles away, on Sunday mornings and there are some who do not attend any service at all.

There is no television in any of the Camphill communities. This stems partly from the fact that as a therapeutically orientated movement, Camphill gets some of the 'casualties' of this medium – children and youngsters whose beings are almost entirely moulded by what they have seen on TV, who virtually have what one might call 'television personalities'. Because they cannot select the programmes which might be constructive, they absorb the violence and pornography along with the rest and can develop pathological motives to the detriment of themselves and others. Television also puts a strain on meaningful relationships, on potential creativity and initiative and, for all its possible informative value, it tends to cultivate apathy by placing the viewer at the receiving end of what should be an active process.

To the area of social activities belong the many groups, such as the land group, the production group, cultural group, work group, reception group, accommodation group, building group and many others. The function of these groups is partly administrative, but they also serve to keep alive the human element of interdependency as well as the ideals underlying the complex life of the village community.

Botton is a most hospitable place; there is hardly a day without visitors. There are the visits from local groups and clubs; official visits from government bodies and social services; visits from doctors and others in the field of special needs from abroad, who wish to see how the Botton village community lives; and visits by social service students doing projects. There are the conferences to which Botton is host from time to time, and there are

'Peter Pan Travel' (Carnival in Botton).

the Open Days which are tremendous events, when thousands of people from far and wide, stream in busloads through the village and experience unique human warmth and reception.

Quite apart from all these community events, there is the active personal social life of the individuals in the village community. There is much visiting from house to house. There is the Coffee Bar in the heart of the village, with a seating capacity for over fifty people, and which has become a vital meeting place. In the pursuit of their own interests, many of the people with special needs go out to nearby towns such as Whitby and Middlesbrough, those who can manage public transport often taking along with them those who can't. Parents and friends visit.

Everyone in Botton is naturally entitled to a holiday and these are spent in a variety of ways. Some people go to their families, some go to one of the other Camphill villages and others may join a group going to a holiday cottage at home or abroad.

There are occasional village retreats, where groups of people with special needs and co-workers from all the villages in Britain go off somewhere together and spend a weekend talking with one another and gaining fresh insights into each other's lives.

CONCLUSION

To conclude, an attempt to convey something of the life of the Botton village community which has served as an archetype for further villages, something would have to be said about the very many people who have helped to create this first village community and about those who have sustained it with their love and have put their whole lives into it. The Village Community has already created a 'mythos' of its own through many an outstanding contribution, but to name all those who have built the Village in many different ways would require a book in itself.

It would, however, be an omission of the first order not to mention one man by name, whose social wisdom, carrying power, human insight and artistic gifts have inspired the village from the beginning, the Reverend Peter Roth, OBE, a founder member of the Camphill Movement and priest of the Christian Community – known simply as Peter to all in the village, in the Movement and to very, very many more.

Peter Roth

The Camphill Village Trust

As the village centres have developed in Britain, many changes have taken place in the Trust itself since it was registered as a Limited Liability Company in 1954. To begin with, the Council of the Trust was the all-controlling body and every detail of life, first at Botton and then at the other centres, was handled centrally. Gradually, however, the pressure of work became too great and the Council delegated some of its powers to an Executive Committee, and then encouraged the Centres themselves to form Local Management Committees which would, in any case, be in a better position to understand local conditions.

By 1968, the growth, development and changes in the different Centres resulted in a policy of almost complete decentralisation. The first steps in implementing this decentralisation were taken in April 1968, when all matters pertaining to local finances were referred to the Local Management Committees, with the obvious result that the central Executive Committee became redundant. Instead, the Local Management Committees became directly responsible to the Council of the Camphill Village Trust.

This move had far-reaching effects, in that the entire system of fund-raising and public relations changed; instead of an organisation run completely by the Council of the Village Trust, groups were formed in direct relation to the centres themselves: 'The Friends of Botton', 'The Friends of Newton Dee', etc now worked in close cohesion with and were responsible to the respective Local Management Committees. In order, however, to retain an image of the Camphill Village Trust, as such, a central committee within the Council became responsible, to some extent, for policies in fund-raising and public relations, as well as for all printed matter.

During the years of the existence of the Camphill Village Trust, other aspects of overall administration were also decentralised, and the different Centres gradually acquired almost complete autonomy. In order to prevent splits or even schisms between the centres, which can be a result of autonomy, if carried to an extreme, sub-committees of the Council were formed to hold all the many threads together. The sub-committees cover such matters as policy, waiting-lists, Counselling Service, finance and the like and are, at the same time, responsible to the Council.

Thus the history of the Camphill Village Trust is one of a progression from centralisation towards individualisation to cooperation. We all feel this to be the right and healthy way of growth, as sustained central control would only result in a stifling of individual initiative and incentive at the centres. A

Basketmaking (The Grange).

differentiated and lively network of functions and responsibilities all over the country obviates a tendency towards control and bureaucracy and, at the same time, maintains the symbiosis of a great variety of initiatives, challenges and conditions in the different Camphill Village communities.

The Camphill Village Trust was registered as a Charity with the Charity Commissioners in 1960.

GRANGE OAKLANDS VILLAGE

The Grange began in 1957 with a view to training young people who would later go on to one of the village communities. With the passing of time, however, it developed into a small village community in its own right. Its thirty-three acres, set on the fertile western slopes of the broad Severn valley, were very conducive to fruit growing, and juice-making and jam-making is a Grange specialty.

Twenty years later in 1977 Oaklands Park, an estate to the South West, was bought by the Trust and ultimately became part of the Grange. Its 120 acres of horticultural/agricultural land and its thirty woodland acres presented extended opportunities, and challenges.

A contemporary description may best be given from a bird's eye viewpoint. The intimate clustering of the Grange houses around its singularly beautiful village hall; the newly-built Therapy house, the basketry, pottery, bakery, fruit-processing and craftwood workshops; its spinney and the pathways meandering through the luxuriant undergrowth – all this contrasts sharply with the central, dominating mansion-house of Oaklands Park with its weavery and, separated by acres of parkland and fields, its two outlying cottages, wood workshop and farm!

Transport is a feature of life in Grange Oaklands with the four–times-a-day shuttling of people to and from their places of work – and to evening groups, talks or social events. Burdensome in many respects, this positive exchange of personnel prevents any tendency of overlooking the virtues which live in either place. There are daily runs to transport a minibus-load of older children to Wynstones School; and there are several deliveries a week to Gloucester of bread and vegetables, and occasional produce runs to supply markets further afield.

The religious life of the community is now well-rooted, through the congregation of The Christian Community.

NEWTON DEE VILLAGE COMMUNITY

In 1945, Newton Dee, a 173-acre estate with mansion house and several cottages and home farm, was acquired by the Camphill Schools at Aberdeen, and run first for delinquent boys, and later for older boys with special needs of training age for whom a variety of workshops was erected. It was at Newton Dee that the first idea of the village community began to germinate and came to fulfilment.

It is a community of 200 people in twenty households of varying size.

Francis House was built to provide a home for those who are elderly or frail and need extra care. The two farms and gardens supply the community with meat, dairy produce and vegetables. The craft workshops – joinery, weavery, batik, metal, soft dolls, textile printing and wooden toys – produce high quality goods. The bakery, confectionery, laundry, village store, coffee bar and gift shop attract much local custom. A village hall, where there are concerts, plays, conferences and other events, includes the wider community; and the proximity to Aberdeen allows easy access to a variety of city attractions. Camphill Architects, whose services are used in Great Britain and parts of Europe, has been situated in Newton Dee since 1977.

DELROW COLLEGE & REHABILITATION CENTRE

By 1963, two needs had prompted the Camphill Village Trust to acquire the Delrow College and Rehabilitation Centre at Aldenham in Hertfordshire, just fifteen miles from Marble Arch in London. On the one hand, the Trust's office in its rented premises in Harley Street had become very cramped. On the other, more and more young people with special needs needed a period of assessment before actually entering a village. Thus Delrow House began.

With the decentralisation of the work of the Trust's office Delrow, while remaining a place of assessment, began to render a unique service to

Copper Metal Workshop (Newton Dee).

people with psychiatric trouble, who come out of hospital for a few months, a few days, even a few hours. For many long-term hospital patients this has meant a new ray of light; for others, the beginning of a path back into the wider community.

In 1965, the College was founded to provide adult education in the widest sense of the word. Lecturers, artists and therapists, from other Camphill centres and from elsewhere, come in to help in the college and a new building has now been erected to accommodate it. Besides this, there are a variety of workshops as well as the gardens. The acreage and the number of houses have both increased over the years.

Delrow is much in the public eye and places for students in social work from Great Britain and abroad and for trainee nurses are constantly in demand. Being so near London, it is the scene of steady coming and going of people from official bodies, hospitals, local authorities and other kindred organisations.

Delrow is also a place of meetings between people from all the Camphill Centres in Britain and a stop-over point for people going to and coming from abroad. Through all this seething movement and change, it is not always the most secluded and restful of places, but it stands as a pillar of tolerance and compassion in the midst of the many needs it endeavours to meet.

CAMPHILL HOUSES STOURBRIDGE

The rural village community setting does not appeal to all people with special needs and there are always those who wish to work in open employment and are capable of doing so, often with a minimal degree of advice and guidance. The difficulty here lies in the fact that such people are not so inclined to protect their own interests. Also they are influenced very much by the circumstances in which they have lived elsewhere. With these needs in mind the first of the Camphill Houses in Stourbridge, near Birmingham, was acquired by the Camphill Village Trust in 1969. Since that time further houses have been purchased to accommodate the needs of the growing community.

People with special needs and co-workers alike contribute to the economic running of the houses by being involved in a variety of jobs and activities. This includes paid employment with local firms, schools, MSC schemes, domestic service and the like, as well as the daily running and maintenance of the houses. Everyone is encouraged to participate in the cultural and leisure activities which the locality has to offer: a church social group, rambling club, folk dance society and a photographic society. Also adult education classes, study groups, concerts and lectures are attended.

After having built up a group of friends and contacts in the locality, many people take further steps towards independence: first, lodging with selected local families under the auspices of Camphill Houses; later perhaps, conventional lodgings or a Council flat. Many of the people with special needs who have moved out of Camphill Houses and now live independently have formed a Fellowship which meets regularly. Its members help and support each other both practically and socially as well as turning their attention and care towards others in need.

THE CROFT COMMUNITY

Founded in 1976, The Croft is an urban community situated in the small market town of Malton in North Yorkshire.

The community comprises four houses within the town itself and one a few miles away. These five houses are home for fifty people. Workshop facilities offered include a café, bookshop, giftshop, gardens, cooking and domestic housework, woodwork, weavery and metalwork.

Living in a community one is quickly made aware of how dependent each of us is on our neighbour. This interdependence and the feeling that everyone is needed helps to develop self-confidence and responsibility. Attributes such as these can help those with special needs to integrate into the wider community. The Croft seeks to create an atmosphere and environment to facilitate this integration, while at the same time providing a secure social environment for its members.

The varied cultural activities and social contacts which a town provides can also be of benefit to those recovering from nervous breakdowns. The challenge of community living in an urban situation can often be a real stimulus on the road to recovery.

LOCH ARTHUR COMMUNITY

Loch Arthur Community lies six miles from Dumfries, the principal town of the largely agricultural South West corner of Scotland. The estate consists of two farms which surround a fine Georgian country house together with two cottages and the well preserved walled garden. The two groups of farm buildings, only one of which included a farmhouse when the Community started, lie half a mile apart at opposite ends of the estate. Including Loch Arthur itself and some woodland there are well over 500 acres. The climate is mild and the landscape one of hills and woods, water and green fields with livestock grazing.

The community began in 1984 as an initiative of the whole Scottish Region of Camphill and with the support of the Camphill Village Trust. The intention was to found an agricultural community that would have ample scope for future growth. It was hoped that work on the land would give a secure and challenging foundation to the community's development, one element of which was clearly imagined to be the integration of some people with severe handicaps into the life of a working rural community.

The first years have seen the beginning of meeting these challenges and balancing these demands. The farm and garden have become productive and rewarding, with sheep, dairy cows and vegetable growing as the main enterprises. A creamery and bakery have been established and the mainly young population has matured in the process of pioneering. The existing houses have been improved and extended and, with the building of a new farmhouse to be completed in 1989, the community will number about sixty-five people living in five houses. The tremendous potential for healing that can be recognised in Loch Arthur and the strength of support for the community in the locality promise well for the future.

Cheesemaker (Loch Arthur)

LARCHFIELD COMMUNITY

The Larchfield Community was established in 1986 after requests from the Middlesbrough Borough Council to the Camphill Village Trust to set up a community within the town's boundary to develop disabled and special employment facilities in a Camphill community setting. This was the result of a visit by a group of officers and councillors of the Middlesbrough Council to Botton Village. They had identified areas of unemployment among people with special needs and were interested in ways to solve the problem.

Work is centred around the land with farm, market garden and estate work as well as a land related workshop in catering and food processing.

Another aspect of the community is the adult education facilities. From the beginning, facilities such as hall and coffee bar provide the space for talks, study groups and practical work with both the resident community and the day workers.

There is a lot of potential in this unique site between the industrial and residential Teesside area and the North Yorkshire hills and moors.

THE COUNSELLING SERVICE

The Counselling Service of the Camphill Village Trust grew out of the endeavour in our centres to help parents to understand the problems of their sons and daughters with special needs and to follow up the path of each person trying to make his or her way into the wider community. These endeavours still continue today, both in our schools and villages and indeed have always been in the nature of what is now termed 'counselling'.

By 1970-71 however, it clearly showed that a group should be available whose *primary* concern was the welfare of our friends who had left a village for whatever reason and for interim counselling for some of those on the waiting lists. A small group drawn from those working in the Trust's centres formed around this task, soon to be joined by others whose life experience had involved them in counselling as well as by a number of interested younger people employed within the social services and with particular interest in Camphill's work.

The group has its focal point at Ringwood in Hampshire from where inquiries for advice and help can be redirected to the appropriate counsellor. Each counsellor works independently and also deals personally with local inquiries.

The therapeutic relationship, which should exist between the one who counsels and the one who is counselled, emphasizes the truth that we need each other in order to deepen our self-knowledge and at the same time to be of greater help to those who call on us in our role as counsellors. Both counsellor as well as counselled must recognise and acknowledge their common humanity with its weaknesses and its strivings and through this recognition foster confidence in this important aspect of the wider work of Camphill.

Over the years the Counselling Service has rapidly developed to meet many outside calls for help. The attempt is made by each member of the group to be available for all calls for help from mentally ill and people with special needs and their families irrespective of their interest in Camphill.

The Counselling Service now embraces a wide horizon and enables Camphill to play an active part in those services offered by the community to its needy fellow human beings.

Recorder Player
(Stourbridge).

OTHER CAMPHILL COMMUNITIES IN
ENGLAND, SCOTLAND AND WALES

CAMPHILL DEVON COMMUNITY

The Camphill Devon Community sits perched on the South-Western edge of Dartmoor, a mile and a half from the small village of Buckfastleigh. Previously a home for diabetic and asthmatic children, Hapstead Village, as it is also known, became a Camphill centre when six co-workers and six villagers from Botton village, as well as twenty adults from local mental hospitals arrived at new year's 1980.

To begin with, the community directed its efforts towards establishing the farm and garden. The community has in total sixty-eight acres of land, of which five acres are garden, twelve acres forest and the rest farm land. A pottery and weavery were established, and a wood workshop, which specialises in bowls, candlesticks and lampstands turned on lathes.

Camphill Devon Community comprises seven units. Three form the main house, whose architecture spans a century, having been built in three instalments; three buildings are a renovated farmhouse, a bungalow and an extended lodge; and a new house was completed in 1986.

Hapstead is also a centre of the Christian Community.

CAMPHILL MILTON KEYNES COMMUNITY

Camphill Milton Keynes is an attempt to integrate a Camphill centre into an urban setting. It is situated on the edge of the new town of Milton Keynes and comprises four households, three acres of horticultural land and a hall/workshop complex containing a weavery, joinery, bakery and food processing unit.

Residents are encouraged to take advantage of outside facilities, culturally and socially, and neighbours attend the festivals.

The community presently totals forty people but this will more than double when a nearby ten acre site has been fully developed.

CAMPHILL COMMUNITY EAST ANGLIA

Situated at Thornage Hall, a delightful listed building in the heart of Norfolk,

Wheel Painter (The Hatch).

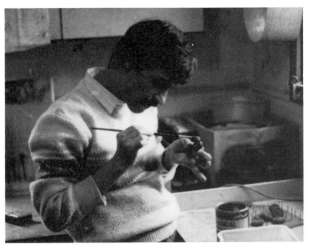

Camphill Community East Anglia will provide a home and community for some thirty-five people when the plans are turned into houses. The very peaceful surrounding will enhance the therapeutic environment which will comprise three houses, workshops and a small forty-seven acre farm.

THE HATCH

The Hatch is a therapeutic community of two houses for young adults with special needs between nineteen and twenty-five years old. It is situated on a separate estate from The Sheiling School (Thornbury) but remains closely affiliated to the school, sharing some facilities and finding common ground in cultural and social activities. Daily working life is independent of the school.

Guided work-experience is offered in landwork, cooking, laundry and other domestic tasks. Organic gardening, woodwork and weaving are also essential activities.

WILLIAM MORRIS CAMPHILL COMMUNITY

This community is named after William Morris (1834-1896), the designer, craftsman, writer, printer, environmentalist and pioneer in architectural preservation. It began in 1978 in Stonehouse, Gloucestershire as a further education centre for adolescents and has since added a small community for adults with special needs.

Workshop activities include weaving, pottery, woodwork, basketry, book-binding, leatherwork, sewing, metalwork, domestic science and landwork.

There is one large house with three subdivisions as well as a farm called Orchard Leigh, the base of the adult community.

SHEILING FARMS COMMUNITY

Folly Farm Lane and Sturts Farm near Ringwood are the two residential and working communities which, at present, constitute Sheiling Farms. They began out of the concern for young adults with special needs and their need to grow into a working life and a social setting adjusted to their capacities. The farm work includes arable cultivation, poultry, pigs and woodland management. Included in the horticultural work is the cultivation of a market garden and plant nursery for bedding plants, herbs and cuttings. There is also a well-equipped bakery, weavery and laundry.

THE MOUNT COMMUNITY

The Mount School Community, located on the Weald of Kent in Wadhurst, East Sussex, provides a home for twelve to twenty year old adolescents. The main house was a Victorian Monastery; there are two other houses and one

Varnishing (The Hatch)

under construction in late 1988 for older college students. Some of the college students do so well in the craft work that they are able to go on to do City and Guilds exams.

CORBENIC COLLEGE

Corbenic College was founded in June 1978 by Thomas and Anke Weihs. The main building was a hunting lodge which had been used by the Rothschild family and the King of Spain, situated on a cliff overlooking the torrential River Braan in the central Scottish highlands.

The community has a markedly seasonal rhythm in that all its members work outside in the small garden and orchard for some part of the day between Easter and Michaelmas, while during the winter most people work indoors in simple craft workshops (weaving, candle making, basket making) leaving only the strongest to continue essential outside work such as sawing logs and snow clearing.

CRAIGMYLE COMMUNITY

Craigmyle has been in existence since 1978 and joined the Association of Camphill Communities in 1987. It is very much accepted in the local Scottish community and involved in events and activities in nearby Banchory. This is especially apparent in the running of their local shop. Craigmyle also works a large garden, runs a smallholding looking after cows, sheep, pigs, goats and poultry, and looks after its own daily household needs. Craigmyle is small with places for five adults with special needs and when time permits extends its support to local elderly people and others through visiting and practical help. Through caring for each other, the animals and local people with needs, everyone at Craigmyle senses that they are needed and grow in dignity.

COLEG ELIDYR

Coleg Elidyr is situated half way up a beautiful Welsh valley. Here, there exists a college of further education for adolescents with special needs and, after a very comprehensive training in crafts and life skills, some young people become apprentices and live in the nearby town of Llangadog helping to run the restaurant or work in the workshops of Victoria House and gaining the confidence to live in society. A farm near Llangadog offers training in farm work and horticulture.

CAMPHILL COMMUNITIES IN
——IRELAND——

Dancers (Mourne Grange)

GLENCRAIG COMMUNITY

Glencraig Community is situated on an estate of ninety-five acres on the Southern shore of Belfast Lough. In 1954 a group of parents in Northern Ireland expressed a strong wish to establish a Camphill school for their children with special needs. Seven years later it became necessary to extend the School, and the Training School for young people (16 to 18 years) was established. Two years later, in 1963, the community acquired the adjoining estate of Craigowen which made it possible to start the Glencraig Village Community for adults. The three year Young Adult Training Scheme for people aged between eighteen and twenty-five was established in 1984 with the aim to give young adults with special needs the opportunity to mature through a disciplined work training and further education. More recently

48

the needs of the ailing and ageing adults with special needs have become more apparent and it was recognised as a task the community should take on. With the establishment of Clanabogan in 1984 and with it the moving out of a number of established villagers, it became clear that the village impulse itself should move from Glencraig, and that the school, training and provision for the older villagers should be the main tasks of the community.

There are fifteen houses, a chapel for the Christian Community, three halls, three school buildings and a swimming pool. The workshops are the farm, garden, laundry, store, domestic work and the weavery.

MOURNE GRANGE VILLAGE COMMUNITY

Mourne Grange Village Community was established in 1971 by a group of people coming from the Glencraig Community. It had formerly been a boys' preparatory school, with a very large house, cottages, outhouses, a chapel and farm. For administrative purposes Mourne Grange Village is a subsidiary company of the Glencraig Trust, a recognised charity.

The community is situated in peaceful rural surroundings in the foothills of the Mourne Mountains, not far from the sea and has the atmosphere of a village in which everyone knows what is happening and is interested and concerned with the life of the place.

From the outset, caring for and working the land at Mourne Grange was felt to be the right basis for the community's endeavours. There is a farm of eighty-three acres, vegetable gardens, an orchard producing soft fruit and an estate workshop. A central laundry and food processing facilities also serve the needs of the community. The products from the large, well-equipped pottery, weaving workshop and wood workshop are sold on their own merit, together with the crafts and gift items from other Camphill centres and elsewhere, in the community's craft shop and tea room, 'Cresset Crafts', at the entrance to the estate.

CAMPHILL VILLAGE COMMUNITY DUFFCARRIG

Camphill Village Community Duffcarrig began in 1972 as a sturdy seedling with a remarkable degree of public interest and mutual contact, when a group of friends and parents of children with special needs, through contact with Glencraig, asked Camphill to establish a centre in the Irish Republic.

Duffcarrig is South of Dublin in a rural area on the East coast next to the sea. It is surrounded by farms and woodland and enjoys a mild climate. It began as one large house but has since purchased adjoining fields and cottages and has built three additional houses on fifty acres of land. Growth has been steady but slow due to the majority of capital funds being from voluntary contributions. More and more capital funding comes from the state thus enabling growth to accelerate.

There is a weaving workshop, a wood workshop and a laundry. Since there are many villagers with very special needs, there is a wish to develop art therapy and curative eurythmy.

CLANABOGAN VILLAGE COMMUNITY

This Camphill place for adults with special needs was founded in 1984 near Omagh, County Tyrone among hills of grass and moor and bordering the Owenreagh River. The gardens and farm are gradually expanding over the fifty-six acres. A new craft workshop, two new houses and a village hall have recently been finished.

CAMPHILL COMMUNITY DUNSHANE

Dunshane House, which is a forty minute drive from Dublin, began in 1985 as a new training college for adolescents in need of special education and care. The Victorian manor house and twenty-six acre stud farm has been transformed into a land-based community with craft workshops and special education. Dunshane means 'The House of John'.

GRANGEMOCKLER CAMPHILL COMMUNITY

In the early 1980s some people from Grangemockler in County Tipperary near the foot of Mt. Slievenamon started looking for a house in which to employ someone to look after their village's socially disadvantaged adults. Seeking professional advice they turned to a social worker who introduced them to Ballytobin and Duffcarrig. After many ups and downs the village committee together with Ballytobin, a Camphill School, found a suitable forty-acre holding. The intention is to turn this property called Temple Michael into a Camphill village community for up to thirty people.

CAMPHILL COMMUNITIES IN
–CENTRAL EUROPE–

Aigues-Vertes Shop in Geneva

AIGUES-VERTES

Since 1961, 'la Fondation Aigues-Vertes' has been a Camphill village community. It is situated on a bend of the Rhone River near the city of Geneva, Switzerland. Power lines from a neighbouring chemicals factory cross the land, the motorway is close by and there is continual air traffic overhead. The village is like a misty oasis in the midst of all this. The silence of the Spring nights is broken by the song of the nightingale and from the bare Winter trees the cry of the barn owl is heard. The cow bells in the meadows around the houses remind one of the distant Alps.

The 128 acres of land are looked after by the gardeners, the farmers, the estate team and the foresters. A large proportion of the village population works in the bakery and the craft workshops: pottery, wool workshop, weavery, wood and metal workshops. Crafts are sold in the

51

village shop and in one of its own shops in the city. But for more and more people participation in productive work is not possible. They are therefore involved in activities of a therapeutic character – eurythmy, Bothmer gymnastics, colour and light therapy. There is also a seminar in Social Therapy.

The Christian Community chapel is nestled against the hillside overlooking the rest of Aigues-Vertes.

FONDATION PERCEVAL

'Fondation Perceval' has been part of the Camphill Movement since 1965. Situated in the vineyards above Lake Geneva, and on clear days offering an inspiring view of the Alps, the school has been in constant expansion in order to meet the needs of children with special needs in French-speaking Switzerland. One necessary step has been the establishment of training, working and living conditions suitable for the adults who were once pupils of the school, the oldest of whom is now over forty.

Cultural life and workshops are centred at Perceval itself, where there is the school, the hall, the main workshop (wood carving, pottery, carpet-knotting and knitting and weavery), the farm and the bookshop, whilst the living units are very much at the periphery, often at a good distance from one another. The farm, Les Biolles, follows the rhythm of the seasons and the inhabitants live very close to nature. L'Hirondelle being very close to Perceval shares intensively in the life of the community. Le Bourg in the mediaeval village of St-Prex contains a shop which sells Camphill products and other crafts as well as newspapers, sweets, etc It is very much a part of all events of the village. Quatre Coeurs, the last born, is the furthest away. A large demesne and part of a rural setting, its inhabitants are largely connected to what goes on in their own locality but most commute to Perceval for at least half of the day. A three-year training course in Social Therapy has been established for co-workers.

HUMANUS HAUS

Humanus Haus is situated within sight (on clear days) of the famous Bernese Alps in Switzerland. The little town of Worb with its tenth century castle is almost two miles away.

The property, with a large old house, a nurse's home, two dilapidated gate lodges and a church yard was taken over in 1973 from the Diakonissen Order who had an old people's home there. In 1975 a

beautiful, large Bernese farmhouse was also acquired. This has been completely rebuilt and houses the joinery, bakery, Choroi-lyre workshop, the bookshop/giftshop, café and a small living unit. On the land around it has been built three living units, a weavery, swimming pool, gardenhouse, greenhouse and the beautiful Humanus-Hall. With the purchase of a large farm in Vielbringen in 1987 the orchards and vegetable gardens can be expanded.

About forty villagers and forty young trainees live together in eleven family units. In the largest of the new houses, Karl-König-Haus, there is a therapy unit including massage/hydro therapy, music therapy, colour-light therapy and eurythmy rooms.

In Humanus-Haus, besides the training course in Social Therapy which many Camphill Villages offer, there are opportunities to learn music therapy and do apprenticeships in bio-dynamic gardening and in cabinet-making.

This all makes for a varied, intensive life, very fitting for the changing groups of trainees and a challenge to all the adults whose tasks it is to maintain a harmonious basis for the many activities.

LE BÉAL

Le Béal, in France, is situated on the windy banks of the Rhone Valley on the edge of Provence. The rural surroundings of the little village of Taulignan are patterned with lavender fields and vineyards and nearby is 'Le Béal', an old silk mill with a small neighbouring farm.

The one single large house-community is being transformed into different households. The farm tries to establish itself into its Mediterranean countryside.

Over the years it became apparent that the fullness and richness of community life is a way of living together and a path of learning out of which springs new social ideas and healing forces. Such a life creates a web of human bonds which enlarges the community far beyond its physical boundaries and makes the effort towards social integration all the more real and active.

LIEBENFELS

It was not until 1976 that a Camphill community started in Austria – the country of Karl König's birth. Liebenfels is in Southern Karinthia, near Klagenfurt, and situated about 2500 feet above sea level. It is very close to

*The Wertsch
(Liebenfels).*

the ruins of a Celtic Temple, which is in the centre of four holy mountains and surrounded by a beautiful landscape of lakes and valleys. It started on rented land in rented houses on a twenty-five year lease. In 1983 a house and almost four acres of land were purchased. But there is very little money for all the building plans. On land between three local villages, there are three farms which have been rebuilt into eight households and workshops. One is still a farm, and there are also gardens, a wool and silk knitting workshop, a weavery, a doll workshop, wood workshop and a bakery.

LEHENHOF

It was due to the initiative of the parents of Nadia Peill-Meininghaus who, from the age of five, had attended the Sheiling Schools in Thornbury, that in September 1964 a small group of co-workers started the Lehenhof. It is located in South Germany, in the Deggenhauser Valley, which lies at an altitude of about 2000 feet. When the weather is really clear one can look down onto the Lake of Constance and glimpse the snow-covered mountain range of the Alps.

A derelict farm formed the nucleus of the community. Now there are two farms, gardens, a community centre with therapy rooms and a nursing ward. The workshops produce bread and other baked goods, woollen underwear, woven goods, rugs and sawmill products – fruit boxes and forklift palettes.

An important aspect of community work lies in the rehearsing for performances of plays, concerts and festivals. All efforts in living and working together and in sharing cultural experiences are directed towards the hope that those people who want to stay in the Lehenhof village community can find a home here.

At present there are twenty-five households with 115 adults in need of special care.

HERMANNSBERG

On a Northern range of hills nine miles from the Lake of Constance in Germany in sight of the Swiss Alps is the Hermannsberg village community. It is the youngest Camphill establishment in this area and yet has the longest

Grape Harvesting
(Le Béal).

history. It is mentioned in historical documents as early as 1254 and in 1360 a Franciscan monastery was founded there. In 1920 the boarding school Schloss Salem bought Hermannsberg as a hostel – the Duke of Edinburgh was one of those taught there. Before Hermannsberg became a Camphill centre in July 1976 it had been standing empty for some years and so all the buildings had to be thoroughly renovated. Some people with special needs came from the Lehenhof and helped with the pioneering work. Even people with very special needs found a place in this community and this, in fact, has been one of the main motives which led to its founding. A very short time later Hermannsberg was able to buy a 100-acre farm, the Lichthof.

The village community comprises ten houses, one of which is a therapy centre where there live two smaller families who concentrate mainly on nursing. In the course of the years a broad spectrum of different work areas has developed with the aim of producing goods which are really needed: furniture, wooden toys, spinning wheels, baskets, knitted and woven garments. A laundry serves the village households and customers in the surrounding district.

Since the emphasis on people with very special needs is in the process of increasing, the whole cultural and therapeutic realm gains in importance. The hall in the old monastery building can only just accommodate everyone. Therefore plans for future expansion include a new community centre.

Netting Fish
(Maartenhuis).

HAUSENHOF

Since 1979 parents and co-workers of the Karl-König School, a day school in Nürnberg, Germany, have worked together to initiate a village for their children. In 1983-84 a seventy-acre farm about thirty-five miles West of the city, and close to the well-known beautiful old town of Rothenburg o.d. Tauber, was discovered and purchased, and in October 1987 the first group of co-workers and villagers moved in.

The Hausenhof, as it is called, is a lonely farm on a hill overlooking the beautiful countryside of the Steigerwald. Hundreds of people completely rebuilt the old farmhouse and improved existing farm buildings, including a byre, pig sty, sheep pen and farm machinery shed. An old stable has become the first workshop, a basketry. In the future it is hoped to renovate a house in the next village and to build more accommodation in order to expand beyond the present population of under twenty people.

MAARTENHUIS

Maartenhuis was founded in 1980 as a place for adults who had outgrown Christophorus, a Camphill School near Zeist in the Netherlands. It had formerly been an Anthroposophical children's home but had lain abandoned for four years and had become a ruin. It is located on the island of Texel, and lies about fifteen minutes walking distance from the sea, sheltered by high dunes. Summers are lovely and sunny, but the winters cold and storm-tossed, with up to gale force winds.

The first co-workers and seven people with special needs who moved in 1980 to Maartenhuis started work with a large-scale rebuilding programme. Now eighteen villagers live in one large wooden house, one stone house, a small wooden hall and holiday huts. There is a mini fifteen-acre farm with cows and sheep, beehives, large gardens, a central wash house, a wood workshop and a weavery with shop attached. It is aimed to build a new house and farm unit.

CAMPHILL COMMUNITIES IN
—SCANDINAVIA—

Autumn in Hogganvik.

VIDARÅSEN LANDSBY

Vidaråsen Landsby was founded at Whitsun 1966, a village community not preceded by the existence of a Camphill school in Norway. In this sense it broke new ground. The village is situated in the county of Vestfold, seventy-five miles South of Oslo, and a little inland from the two coastal towns of Sandefjord and Tønsberg. The landscape is forest terrain with hills and valleys. Summers are short but sunny. Autumn with its coloured leaves has clear and rainy days. The snow covers the ground from December until April and Spring comes like an explosion.

At the outset Bakke Gård was bought – a little farm with eight acres of land and thirty-five of forest.

The first village family house was begun on the proceeds of charity-sales of candles made by people with special needs and friends of the village. These were arranged by students from Oslo and Vestfold. Another fourteen houses followed, all built of timber in a traditional Norwegian style. Ita Wegman Hus is increasingly becoming a nursing unit, with a sick room, and facilities for therapeutic baths and massage. The Andreas Chapel and the Kristoffer Hall are public buildings.

In 1984-85 a double glazed greenhouse was constructed, and now a new farm building is being added. The forestry work is to a large extent that of clearing and tidying. Timber from the forest has been used in many of the village buildings. Repeated attempts have been made to plant fruit bushes – only time will tell whether it has been worth the effort.

The bakery is at bursting point and a larger one is being considered. Next door is a pottery which was enlarged in 1985. The joinery has been

Silage making (Tapolan).

making wooden toys for many years and the doll workshop makes a larger doll and two baby dolls.

Like many other Camphill centres, Vidaråsen has a wide ranging cultural life. Unique about Vidaråsen is its forty-five-member string orchestra consisting of villagers, co-worker children and some co-workers.

HOGGANVIK LANDSBY

Hogganvik was started in 1972 as the second village community in Norway. It is situated on the West coast where nature is unpredictable and has a strong influence on people. In order to take the place in hand, it has been necessary to rebuild and reshape it. It has been quite a task to tame and humanise the land. Only twenty-five acres out of 190 are arable. There is a farm, vegetable garden and weaving workshop. The large forest also provides work in the Winter time. In the surroundings, one sees the wrestling between the new and the old, represented by the oil business amidst a very conservative rural population.

JØSSÅSEN LANDSBY

Jøssåsen Landsby started as a Camphill village in 1978 at the request of parents from the area around Trondheim, Norway, which is about a one hour's drive away. It is situated by a lake at the foot of a hill. The surrounding hills are covered with fairy-tale-like forests. This lovely landscape is very little touched by man.

The community has five houses plus a weaving workshop. The farm has cattle and sheep and the garden includes a heated greenhouse. The cutting of firewood is a year-long task. During the berry season, common effort is made at harvesting the blueberries, raspberries and cranberries.

VALLERSUND LANDSBY

Vallersund was established in response to the need to provide community life for people with drug problems, and an adventurous group of people with special needs have since joined the community. It includes three households with two more on the way, for there is a long waiting list.

It is situated about two hours from Trondheim by boat out to the coastline or by ferry and car. There, close to the sea, where the tide rises and recedes and often strong winds sweep the country, lies Vallersund Farm. Once it was a trading place, also a harbouring home for seafarers. Farming and candlemaking are also part of daily life. Historically, it is situated near ancient standing stones and recently one of Norway's first windmills was erected nearby.

In the first three years life was a great struggle, asking a lot of those who stood it through. Drug addicts came as revolutionaries to all fundamental ideas of Camphill and the test was hard. But in the end Camphill life in its fundamental task to restore the dignity of man seemed after all to have a healing effect. Nevertheless, great stress still lies on those who carry the work. It is an immense challenge and presents the trial of self-education that makes people. Vallersund is a challenge for those who want to stand face to face with the shadow existence of our time.

SOLBORG/ALM

Solborg, founded in 1977, was established as a training centre for young people from fourteen to eighteen years of age. Alm was founded as a living situation for adults with special needs in 1983. The two properties lie on a hillside, with approximately five minutes walk between them. The climate is typical of South East Norway with cold Winters and often dry Summers.

There are seven houses, a barn and a new workshop building at Solborg with a joinery, metal workshop and mechanics workshop, as well as a weavery and candle workshop. There are twenty-eight arable acres, 150 acres of forest.

Cooperation between Solborg and Alm is complicated by the fact that the trainees, many of whom suffered a very deprived childhood, are too immature to be sufficiently understanding of the older villagers. But lately the two groups have mixed better and a healthier living together seems possible.

A therapy group meets regularly to organise individual music therapies and therapeutic painting, as well as to give advice and help to houseparents or workmasters who have difficulties.

TAPOLAN KYLÄYHTEISÖ

Tapolan kyläyhteisö is situated near the town of Lahti in Finland about twenty miles from Sylvia-koti (a Camphill School). The community is right in the middle of the rural village of Niinikoski, which makes integration into the surrounding society quite natural.

Tapolan kyläyhteisö was founded in 1974 when it became necessary to provide the opportunity of village life for young adults who had finished their schooling at Sylvia-koti. Tapola, a farm of sixty acres, was rented and the land was the main source of work in the early days. As the village grew, so craft workshops became necessary and at present, besides farm and garden, there is a weavery, doll workshop, joinery and bakery.

The close proximity of Tapola and Sylvia-koti has enabled the sharing of various cultural events, which will no doubt increase in the future since the completion of the new Hall at Sylvia-koti.

STAFFANSGÅRDEN/MICKELSGÅRDEN

In 1974 a group of young people and co-workers from a health pedagogical institute in Stockholm moved to the outskirts of Delsbo with the intention of founding a Camphill village in the North of Sweden. Here forest-covered hills and mountains surround the two Dellen Lakes. The Winter season is naturally very long and full of snow, but in the Summer the light pours down and at night the stars cannot be seen through the twilight. The folk music is still very alive here and at the festivals people still wear folk costume.

A small hotel, which had formerly been a large farm, and three houses were repaired and renovated and a wood workshop and a little bakery started. The wood workshop produces the Staffan candle holder, named after a well-known Christmas Carol: 'Here rides Staffan with the star on his grey horse followed by two red and two white horses.' (Staffan is a Hälsinglands apostle who brought the Christian message and died a martyr's death here.)

Seven years later another farm was bought just over a mile outside the village – Mickelsgården. This farm made it possible to start accommodating adults. The farm now has sheep, chickens and a horse. The vegetable garden is steadily growing. The forests provide a lot of work in Wintertime.

Membership of the Camphill Movement came about in Autumn 1983.

——— CAMPHILL COMMUNITIES IN ———
NORTH & SOUTH AMERICA

Bookbinders (Copake).

CAMPHILL VILLAGE USA

In 1959, a small group of members of the Camphill community in Scotland went to the United States in answer to a call to continue the work for children with special needs at a little school in Pennsylvania, the directors of which had to retire owing to illness. Camphill in America struck strong roots. Concerned about the future of their sons and daughters with special needs, a group of parents met with Dr. König during one of his visits to America. Through their initiative, a suitable place for starting a village community was found. Another group of Camphill people sailed from the British Isles to America, and on September 17, 1961 Camphill Village USA, Inc. in Copake in upper New York State began its existence. Expansion and development were swift.

The small town of Copake sits in the foothills of the Berkshire Mountains, in a landscape of hills and valleys with many lakes and waterways. Camphill Village occupies 604 acres of land in a small, densely wooded valley. In this area of the United States, Summer is hot and humid, Spring and Fall are splendid, Winter can be hard.

The village has a dairy farm, vegetable and berry gardens, an orchard, solar greenhouse and lots of mixed forest. There are thirty-three major buildings: living units, office, farm buildings, workshop buildings – batikshop, candleshop, bookbindery, enamelshop, weavery, dollshop, bakery and co-op – a doctor's office plus health care unit, gift shop and Fountain Hall – the centre of the community. The buildings, as is the custom in this part of the world, are mainly of wood.

For the co-workers there is a Seminar in Social Therapy which aims to be three years long and for the villagers there is the so-called Village Seminar, conducted once a week.

CAMPHILL VILLAGE KIMBERTON HILLS

Camphill in America received a remarkable legacy in the form of a 345-acre estate in Pennsylvania, complete with a large mansion house, many other smaller houses, a herd of forty-five pedigree Guernseys, farm buildings and equipment. A group moved to Kimberton Hills in the Autumn of 1972. To

Rose Hall (Kimberton Hills).

the original gift, Kimberton Hills first added ten acres and recently an adjoining farm of seventy-eight acres, purchased to protect it from the development now prevalent in this area, where farming is giving way to suburbs. Situated in rolling fields and more than sixty acres of woodland, there is a dairy farm, gardens, orchard, vineyard and sheep pasture. Pfeiffer House and Rose Hall have been built by the Camphill Architects group. The workshops include a bakery, weavery, pottery and a cheese-producing dairy. Cooperation with the nearby Orion Guild House has widened the opportunities to do crafts – woodworking, carving, weaving and leatherwork. The coffee shop and farm store, which sells bread, cheese, milk and vegetables and makes deliveries to local health food stores, are open three days a week.

Kimberton Hills has a three-year Agricultural Training course and the wide circulation of the Kimberton Hills Agricultural Calendar has attracted land-oriented people. A Social Therapy seminar is a more recent development.

TRIFORM

Triform, a Camphill centre for young adults with learning disabilities, is situated on eighty acres in the Hudson Valley in New York State, only twenty minutes away from Copake. The first seven years of trying to establish an economically viable enterprise have been concluded. Triform offers an orientation course of several years in wood working, weaving, pottery making, baking, agriculture and such self-help skills as cooking, laundering, cleaning and learning to live together. In 1986-7 a new community centre was built with two classrooms and a weaving shop. There is space for nineteen students and there are altogether forty-two souls.

CAMPHILL SOLTANE

Camphill Soltane began in 1988 on a twenty-five acre property close to Camphill Special Schools Beaver Run in Pennsylvania. It is a life-sharing community geared toward the young adult between 18 and 25 years.

CAMPHILL VILLAGE MINNESOTA

Situated in the heartland of America, in the midst of what is still the mainstay of American agriculture, Camphill took over a 200-acre dairy farm along the Sauk River, eight miles north of Sauk Centre in October 1980. The purpose:

65

*Geometric Drawing
(Adult Education at
Triform).*

to establish a Camphill Village in response to a request by Minnesota legislators, interested parents and concerned friends who had met the work of Camphill in Copake two years earlier.

The pioneers found themselves among people of German, Polish and Scandinavian descent, many of whom had not learned English until their teenage years, and still retain their original accents. Being familiar with the challenges and tasks that rural life entails, the Camphill co-workers slipped in fairly easily. Since building up a village demands at least two households, a used mobile home was bought and set up next to the original house. Having taken over the fifty-six head Guernsey herd, a start was made in making a living by farming. The farm, which is on black sand soil, had been farmed without artificial fertilisers by the previous farmer for thirty-three years.

The exposure to the extreme weather conditions that are part of the climate of this vast continent is a constant reminder of the immense powers that underlie the forces of growth and decay. These forces of nature provide man with tangible evidence of his place among greater powers, in the face of which few attitudes are more helpful than a certain piety or awe. In winter, temperatures may drop to $-30°F$ ($-34°C$), with winds of 30 to 40 miles per hour. Summer brings fierce thunderstorms which in themselves can bring hail, damaging high winds and tornadoes (thankfully, the tornado zone is generally South of here).

The rhythms of the day, in home life and work in the workshops and on the land present incentives for continual growth in skill, responsibility, self-respect and a meaningful life. Weekly meetings of the whole village afford opportunities for sharing concerns individuals may have, for planning festivals, and for discussing further steps that the community is challenged to take. These meetings, where each person is taken as seriously as the next, are opportunities for soliciting interest, as well as providing incentive for further actions of all involved.

Since its inception in the Autumn of 1980, Camphill Village Minnesota has built two new homes, upgraded its dairy barn to Grade A, built several farm buildings including a heated farm workshop, and a building which houses an assembly room, bakery, offices and a small weavery.

CAMPHILL VILLAGE ONTARIO

In early winter 1985 a 279-acre property about sixty miles North of Toronto, Canada was discovered which seemed to welcome a Camphill village. Its forests, ravines, marshy areas, varied fields and the fast flowing Nottawasaga River cutting across the corner of the land seemed to offer a balance and quality of environment which could support a community.

Winters are cold and the sun reflecting off the white snow-covered fields can be blinding. In Spring the flowers make an intricate carpet before the leaves shade the forest floor. Summers are often hot. In Autumn the leaves, especially the sugar maples, turn yellow, orange and fiery red.

In February 1986 the first young adult left a nearby anthroposophical curative school and home, followed by four others over the course of the next eight months to join the six young graduates from the school at Rockland Acres. In March 1986 the land was purchased through the generous support of Cawthra and Julyan Mulock, who had first requested that a Camphill be started in Ontario almost twenty-one years before. On May 17th 1986 the Camphill Association of North America officially recognized 'Camphill Village Ontario Inc.'

The present population of over thirty people live in four houses plus a trailer (caravan). Some work at cutting trails through the bush and chopping firewood; others work in a weavery and candle workshop. The property is now over 300 acres, of which about 135 are arable, and it is hoped to begin bio-dynamic farming and gardening in the near future on the loam and sandy soil. It is also hoped that the woodworking skills presently being utilised for renovation and remodelling can eventually be turned to commercial use in a wood and furniture workshop.

So much was allowed to stream towards this tiny beginning and now the seed is bursting into full life.

ANGAIÀ CAMPHILL DO BRASIL

The name chosen to bring the impulse of Camphill to Brazil and actually to South America, *Angaià*, means in Brazilian Indian language, healthy soul.

The work started in 1979 when some children and adolescents joined the first co-workers in three fairy tale like houses at 'A Toca'. Feeling that the greatest need of the country would be for the adults, Angaià moved in September 1981 to the neighbourhood of Juiz de Fora, a city of 800,000 people about two hours drive North of Rio de Janeiro.

The village is located on a sixty acre farm in a region of gentle valleys, about six miles from the town and about 2600 feet above sea level. Workshops include a weavery, wood workshop, candle workshop and herb drying place. The vegetable garden and farm with dairy cattle make the greatest demands upon work. For although nature gives the blessing of planting all year round, nature also brings the extremes of drought and rain, including terrible hailstorms and ants which can destroy in a short time the work of months.

In Brazil there is no support for the handicapped from the government so that even being a charity, Angaià still has to charge parents and relations for the villagers to stay. Sponsorships and donations have been collected in and out of the country making it possible that the impulse develops and grows. Many hands have worked to make it possible for the few hands here to transform this little piece of the world.

CAMPHILL COMMUNITIES IN
——— AFRICA ———

A family from Botswana

CAMPHILL VILLAGE ALPHA

Alpha grew out of the Camphill School at Hermanus, which opened in 1951. A group of residents there reached adulthood and needed the wider opportunity of village life. The village started its independent existence in September 1965 on two farms (one called 'Alpha') bought the previous year, thirty miles North of Cape Town.

     The village is situated on 600 acres, and has sixteen households, a complex of workshops, a community centre and a chapel. There is also a developing farm which is bravely transforming the sandy soil into pastures and crop-bearing fields, though close by are ranges of hills and mountains; these form the surrounding landscape on three sides, and there is the sea on the fourth.

     The climate is a relatively dry one. The average annual rainfall is

69

twenty inches a year; and this means that considerable resources are devoted to irrigation, whilst ecological research has to strive to find crops that can survive with the minimum amount of water. Pilot projects have been started to grow herbs and certain unusual but valuable crops like jojoba, lucerne trees and amaranth that yield essential oils.

The nearness of Cape Town makes it possible to have a lively relationship with this city and to engage in many activities centred there. South Africa is a society in vigorous transition. The ecological, economic, social and political problems that exist in the world are found here in concentrated form. The village is involved in a constant exploration of ways to become open to all population-groups; but this means, inter alia, to overcome the cultural differences that, during the last sixty to eighty years, have inhibited the full-hearted cooperation between members of the various population groups. The residents come from all over South Africa, and some from Namibia and Zimbabwe as well.

The village can therefore not be inward-looking, but has to see itself as part of an evolving pattern in which some of the most intractable problems of our time have to be experienced acutely and tackled urgently.

CAMPHILL FARM COMMUNITY HERMANUS

Camphill Farm Hermanus was established in 1976 to fill the increasing need for adult centres in South Africa. It is situated in the picturesque Hemel en Aarde Valley outside the coastal town of Hermanus, eighty-four miles from Cape Town.

Its first task was to clear trees and bushes to create an area where houses and workshops could be built. The buildings are very attractive architecturally, the old Cape Dutch style being very versatile and fitting well to the landscape.

Farming activities mainly centre around the herd of twenty or more cows. Tending and upgrading of pastures requires tremendous efforts and skilful management on the typically 'thin' South African soil. A lot of cheese is sold through various outlets in the Cape Town area. A small flock of sheep occasionally supplies wool and meat. The vegetable garden is beginning to take shape and is moving towards supplying needs all the year round – a tricky management problem. The herb garden is a source of great pride. A beautiful new workshop has recently been built where the high quality medicinal and culinary herbs are dried, stripped and packaged.

The wood workshop produces high quality modular pine furniture and can hardly cope with the orders. The recently established pottery is now getting into production with a range of stoneware dishes and planters. The gift shop sells Camphill crafts from all the Southern African Camphill centres.

Groceries for the estate are brought in and sold in the Distribution Store, which is opened once a week for the villagers – a popular social occasion!

CRESSET CAMPHILL COMMUNITY

Cresset House was originally opened by Dr. König in 1961; it was re-established as a centre for children and trainees. It comprised about sixty-five pupils and staff, had six living units, school houses and workshop facilities on a twenty-one-acre piece of land. In 1987 it was handed over to a group of co-workers who are using and transforming this base as a therapeutic community for adults. Its aim is to give a home to about sixty adults and co-workers. A large number of Cresset House pupils were taken on by the adult centre as they had matured into adulthood and needed a Camphill place.

At this point the work concentrates on the land, transforming it into pastures for a small herd of cows; the vegetable garden is to provide for the various house communities. There is a spinning and knitting workshop trying to turn out quality products to be proud of selling on the open market and a bakery selling wholesome bread.

Cresset Camphill Community is situated between two main cities of the Republic of South Africa: Johannesburg and Pretoria. The nearest village or suburb is Halfway House, a place with a lot of small industries where some of the people can have the experience of work in the 'outside'.

This is to all intents and purposes the right answer to the present future need of Camphill's work in South Africa.

NOVALIS HOUSE

Novalis House is situated on a smallholding of nine acres, beautifully wooded and ideal for further development next to an old main road, west of Halfway House between Pretoria and Johannesburg.

Novalis House is a community for children, adolescents and adults, but also has an open ear and a helping hand for black friends in the proximity. To help in this task, there are many therapeutic activities – eurythmy, painting, modelling and singing as well as the daily necessities like cows, garden, estate work, repairs and house work.

CAMPHILL COMMUNITY RANKOROMANE

Rankoromane in Otse, Botswana, is a Camphill Community combining School and Production. Society in Botswana, represented by government, is not able to support the most essential social services. Therefore, the community has chosen to build up workshops employing local people which would support the school with income from their work.

The residential school has forty-two children, ranging in age from seven to eighteen years, mainly mentally handicapped, who live in seven groups in five houses. Cooking is done in two of the houses. They follow an adapted version of the Waldorf curriculum with special emphasis upon the cultural-historical background of Southern Africa, especially African fairy tales and mythology.

The production sector consists of a furniture factory, toy-workshop, textile workshop, horn articles and dolls. There are also gardens and chickens. Due to the drought, all the cattle had to be sold and a planting scheme for over 2000 citrus trees, mainly oranges, was started. The production sector is self-governing with an absolute minimum of hierarchy and a maximum of participation in all levels of decision-making.

Apart from two shops in Otse, there is a rented shop in Gaborone, the capital. The income from the shops support forty-five families.

*The Woodwork Shop
at Rankoromane.*

Botton's Chapel

–CHRISTIANITY IN THE VILLAGES–

In attempting to describe the religious life in a Camphill Village Community, we would first have to say something about the part played by daily work. None of the work in a village – farming, gardening, housework, baking, crafts and the like – is done for the upkeep of the individual. Everyone in a village knows more or less clearly that through all this work, the life of the whole village is maintained, and this, in turn, provides the basis of life for the individual. Thus, people in the villages do their work out of a different incentive from those who work for their personal livelihood. This attitude to work contributes in a fundamental way to a sense of fulfilment in life and, therefore, creates a different relationship to the task in hand.

In what way does work help to fulfil the lives of those with special needs in the villages? Whatever the specific handicap of a person may be, there is, for the most part, a deep gap between his intentions and his means of carrying them out. It is a discrepancy between plan and instrument. Left

73

to their own devices, most people with special needs would spend their time going for bicycle rides, listening to the radio, watching television, or just lounging about. This has little to do with laziness; it is rather an expression of an inability to set themselves in motion. When, however, work is put in their way, they are activated by the demands of their particular task and, moreover, it is they themselves who have to *do* the work; and here deep powers come into play which help to overcome their apparent laziness.

Every person has an intrinsic longing to be a member of society. This longing is not merely a psychological one; it is inherent in the make-up of the human being as are his abilities to walk, to speak, to think. It is a spiritual force and, because it is, it is also a religious force with temporal as well as spiritual implications.

The temporal aspect of being included in society is work. Our people with special needs work because they know that were they not to do so they would fall out of the social order. In fact they will have done so before coming to our villages, where they then hope to heal the breach between themselves and human society. The moment a person with a special need finds something he can do with a degree of excellence, he can become integrated into the life of the community. From being a dispensable entity, he becomes a needed member of his social order. From being a spoilt, selfish, overgrown, over-protected child, he becomes a mature person able to take himself seriously.

But it is not only through his work that a person participates in the infinite give-and-take of the human condition. The spiritual aspect of being a member of society is that every individual is on his way from the Fall of Man to the Redemption of Man through Christ, and here all men are united in a brotherhood of mutual human understanding.

*   *   *

A further, existentially Christian experience comes through the cultivation of knowledge of the world we live in and this is fostered by all kinds of cultural pursuits in the villages. Everyone can participate according to his abilities in folk dancing, singing and acting. And everyone can, again according to his capacities, take in lectures on geography, geology, botany, zoology, astronomy or on the development of man, on politics and art, literature and philosophy. The understanding of such subjects is far less dependent on intellectual ability than is generally thought, and people with special needs particularly have an immediate and unbiased ability to grasp essentials. Thus, adult education in the villages opens windows on to the world, and this can become a religious experience.

All this is gathered up and affirmed by the Communion Service and other Sacraments of the Christian Community. The Christian Community is a movement for religious renewal, founded in 1922 with the help and advice of Rudolf Steiner. The movement began when a group of ministers, theologians and others, disappointed in the existing Churches, but fired with enthusiasm for the new possibilities opened up by Spiritual Science, turned to Rudolf Steiner for guidance. It was through him, but not *by* him, that the Seven Sacraments – Baptism, Confirmation, Marriage, Communion, Confession, Ordination and the Last Rites – were re-established, and The Christian Community was founded. Since then, the movement has been growing steadily and there are Christian Community centres in Britain, in most European countries, and in America, Africa and Australia.

The Communion Service is the most central of the sacraments and it is celebrated every Sunday. Many of the people with special needs have learned to serve at the altar.

*　　*　　*

In order to build a bridge between the Communion Service and the daily life of the village inhabitants, there are talks, both individual and in groups about the sacraments, and a weekly Gospel study on the passage to be read on the coming Sunday. The difficulty in building this bridge lies not only in the non-intellectuality of those with special needs, but also in the over-intellectuality of ourselves. Whereas *we* feel that with sufficient concepts and theories we have comprehended a thing, they are ill at ease with concepts and theories and comprehend things often by much more immediate means. A meeting of these two ways along the path of religious endeavour is always precious, and beneficial to all those who work in a village whatever their standing may be.

Religious life in the village communities is most enhanced by the celebration of the seasonal festivals which are like beautiful, multi-coloured windows looking into a transcendent world. The Act of Consecration of Man, the Communion Service of the Christian Community, plays an important part in the festivals, its seasonal prayers expressing the essence of Michaelmas, Advent, Christmas, Epiphany and Easter. In addition, there are plays and pageants to mark the festivals, each festival having its own customs. Thus, the course of a year in nature and in human existence becomes meaningful and not a mere string of minor events.

Apart from all this, there are many events in the lives of those who constitute a village community: there are the weddings, the Christenings, the funerals – epic moments which are wonderfully supported by all the inhabitants of the village and which become festivals of human love and human regard.

It is in this way that we try to bring Christianity back into the daily life of the community.

*Andreas Chapel
(Vidaråsen).*

ECONOMICS AND MONEY
——IN THE VILLAGES——

Coffee Bar Yard (Botton)

The principle underlying the economic practices in Camphill centres is based on the 'Fundamental Social Law' formulated by Rudolf Steiner in his essays on *Anthroposophy and the Social Question* (1905/6) which we rephrase here:

'The well-being of a community of people working together will be the greater, the more the individual makes over to his fellow-workers the proceeds of his labour – and allows his own requirements to be met out of the proceeds of the work done by others.'

This means that in a group, community or team (Rudolf Steiner was thinking in terms of industry) which tries to put this 'law' into practice, each individual receives what he needs from the community, irrespective of the type and amount of work he does, and that the income derived from the total amount of work achieved by the community is the source from which the individual needs are met.

In applying this idea to concrete situations, it follows that work ceases to be a marketable commodity which can be bought and sold, and that, although it is an instrument for economy, work is primarily a human birthright and a matter of human rights.

With rising unemployment today, the actual monetary situation of people who have been laid off can be on a par with (and sometimes a little better than!) that of those who have jobs, owing to our system of social securities and compensations. At the same time, the moral situation of the unemployed is distressing, to say the least, because work is a human prerogative, and a means of fulfilment which seems to be essential to the dignity and meaningfulness of the human condition. A feeling for the fact that work is a human prerogative to be generously exercised is discernible in today's youth, a considerable number of whom are open to any kind of work as long as it can remain voluntary and not remunerative.

In 1919, in the wake of the disasters of the First World War, Rudolf Steiner presented an outline for a 'Threefold Social Order' to some of the leading and more enlightened statesmen of the time, who recognised its potential as a remedy for social and economic ills. The foundations of the Second World War however, were already being laid and ideas for a constructive and wholesome Europe had to give way. It remains for small communities, if they so wish, to work out their affairs according to this idea of a threefold social order in seed-form, prior to later germination on a broader scale.

In his Threefold Social Order, Rudolf Steiner postulated three distinct spheres in the life of a nation:

Spiritual and Cultural Life
Human Rights and Laws
The Economic Sphere

The principle governing the spiritual and cultural life of a nation would be *freedom* from party-politics, financial convenience and the like. The principle governing the sphere of human rights would be *equality*; there cannot be one set of rights for one class or group of people and another set of rights for another group or class. The laws made to regulate the affairs of a nation must pertain to all. And the principle governing the sphere of economy would be *brotherliness* in the realisation that no man is self-sufficient, that exploitation of others is anti-human and that all men, groups or nations constitute an ecological whole which, if established and maintained as a principle, makes for social health, incentive and satisfaction.

In speaking of the sphere of economy, Rudolf Steiner maintained that man's welfare in the real sense of the word will increase only in proportion to a decrease in his egoism. It would seem that we are proving

Rudolf Steiner

© VERLAG AM GOETHEANUM, Dornach/CH

the validity of this statement every day, for in our competitive society, everyone is in search of his own security, his own welfare and his own status in life and has allowed his egoism to unfold to such an extent that whole cities and nations are going bankrupt, while huge consortiums make astronomical profits, and in the general insatiability for money, fraud, both spectacular and insignificant, has become a way of life. Recently, someone suggested that when future historians look back upon our present period, they will call it the 'Money Culture'.

Although one might say that the Camphill village communities seem, superficially, to be only one among many types of provision for people with special needs, these things have a peculiar relevance, when it comes to the question of integrating the person with special needs into 'normal' society. For broadly speaking, people with special needs do not only lack mental or intellectual acuity; they are also lacking in the ruthless pursuit of their own advantage. This can be and is regarded as a weakness requiring protective measures. It can also be regarded as that more immediate access many people with special needs, untroubled by over-sophistication, have to realities of human existence.

With all this as a background, it is understood by all in the Camphill villages that no wages are paid, but that everyone, including co-workers, contributes to the maintenance of the community as a whole through the particular kind of work he or she does and that personal needs are met as from the total income of the community. The general attitude to the diverse kinds of work in a village – the crafts, workshops, store, farms, gardens, domestic work, etc – is: I do what is needed by others, and they meet my needs.

We would regard the question of needs as belonging to the sphere of Rights rather than to Economy. All human beings have needs and have the right to have their needs met. This, however, does not say that everyone has the same needs. Some individuals, with special needs or otherwise, are monkish in their needs and sackcloth with or without ashes suffices! Others are more demanding. The needs of older people are not necessarily greater than those of younger people, but they are certainly very different. People of all ages can be more gregarious than others and experience their needs fulfilled in the fulfilment of others. Some people might be more introspective and cultivate hobbies or studies which in turn benefit the community, but which have to be invested in. The attitude of some people towards their own belongings is one of transience; others have a greater sense of the value and permanence of objects. There is a veritable universe of variations in the sphere of personal needs, with some basic and common ones such as 'board, lodging and clothing'.

The workshops in the Camphill village communities have all been planned to produce articles of a high standard of workmanship and design which are in demand on the open market without any description of having been made by people with special needs or in aid of charity. The doll workshop at Botton village, one of the first workshops to be established, has produced dolls by the hundreds, which have been sold to leading toy shops the world over. There is a division of labour here, with each of the twenty or so employed having his or her specific job – machinist, cutter, hand-sewing, plaiting doll's hair, making clothing, dressing the dolls and the like. No one person completes a whole doll, but all take pride in the finished product, know what shops have placed orders and are aware of the implications of participation in a production-line.

The incentive to work, as we have indicated, is the pleasure taken in the task at hand and the dignity that accrues to the individual in knowing that his work is not merely something to keep him occupied but is vitally needed.

All workshops in the village communities are organised in a similar fashion to the doll workshop in Botton, with obvious variations dictated by the type of product. The division of labour gives to each worker the chance to find that specific job at which he can excel within his own scope of ability, whilst making a necessary contribution to the finished product, which principle applies to land and household as well.

The income of a Camphill village community is comprised of the following monies: the three Camphill villages in Britain are recognised by the Manpower Services Commission and a Deficiency Grant is paid in respect of each member with special needs registered with the commission as a Disabled Worker in Sheltered Workshops. Further, there is the surplus from the farms, gardens and workshops. Together with the Deficiency Grants, this may be regarded as money earned by the entire community, whereby it should be stated that workshop masters, senior co-workers or any kind of expert, are not subsidised by the Camphill Village Trust, but live from the earned money of the community.

As things are at the present time, neither the Deficiency Grant nor the surplus from land and workshops is sufficient to cover the cost of living,

John Sartain buttering rolls in Botton Bakery.

and it is the interest of both villages and various Local Authorities that the latter make a small maintenance contribution, until such time as the productivity of workshops and land once again replaces it. Other Camphill Village Trust communities depend for some of their income on Local Authority and Department of Health and Social Services grants.

There is also the money received by way of gifts and donations which is, in contrast to money earned, money freely given. Given money is used, as it were, for unproductive projects such as village halls, chapels, social centres and the like. The very nature of such projects presupposes that the use to which they are put is not economically productive.

Finally, there is 'loan money'. In theory at least, dwelling houses can be built from borrowed money, as the people using these houses may be presumed to be earners, and the cost of such loans, including interest, should be met by earned money. Such costs are, in fact, rent and so roughly belong to a normal revenue expense. To some extent, this has been achieved in the centres of the Village Trust, but so far only interest can be met from revenue and capital repayment still has to come from donations.

So much for the way in which Camphill centres regard and try to deal with money and to discern the different purposes to which different kinds of money should be put. Many people have queried Camphill's approach to the wage-question, arguing that in such a system, no one need handle money or be responsible for it, that everything comes from Big Brother and that Camphill communities are glorified mini-welfare-states, in themselves unworldly. There is, no doubt, the danger of all this resulting from Camphill's way of dealing with money. There can be folly in pursuing ideals without being aware of the pitfalls.

Basically, a community must be regarded as being composed of the individuals who live within it. There can be no community without the single people who form the community. It is, therefore, necessary to make sure that every person in the community has a definite standing within it, which means also that he carries responsibility for the whole. This is made possible in the centres through the fact that there is no head, no top executive with a pyramid below of people with diminishing responsibilities. All aspects of life in the villages are the responsibility of various groups who are answerable in their specific area to the whole. These groups are open to any person with special needs in a village who may feel he can help to carry these specific responsibilities.

The largest spenders among these groups are the various households, to each of which is allocated a sum of money from the total earned money of the village community. It is in the different households

Irish musician and singers (Mourne Grange).

that the needs of the individuals are recognised and met. This applies to co-workers as well as those with special needs. But here it is necessary for the individual to cultivate a sense of perspective in relation to his own needs and a feeling of responsibility for the whole house as an economic unit. This is essential to maturity and adulthood. Some people with special needs never really achieve a 'sense' of money and its value; others have it to a high degree, but between the two extremes, everyone in a village receives money to handle, sometimes in the form of a cash account, sometimes in the form of a fixed sum of pocket money, according to individual requirement and ability to cope.

The above is a brief indication of some of the ideals that lie behind the non-wage system, the attitude to work and money and their practical application characteristic of all the Camphill centres. We walk a path of exploration and find that the path has to change to meet different circumstances. But there is the one unchanging factor of search for a deeper understanding of man's relationship to his fellows, to work, to money, to himself.

——CONCLUSION——

The seed that was planted at Botton in 1955 has grown into a strong and viable organism and has seeded itself out over a considerable part of the earth. It has provided places of work and life for people with special needs who might otherwise have been confined to limited scopes of existence. Beyond that, it has provided an experience of a new way of life, of new hope and ideals to a great number of searching young people who had begun to despair of the social trends of our society.

The forms of social life and work that have been developed in these Camphill communities may be relevant to the needs of our society in general. It is widely known that the present trends in society, which are based on maintaining continuous growth, cannot go on indefinitely and that they will have to be relieved by stable forms of society based on moderation. While this is principally accepted, it is as yet, apparently, not possible for any society even to consider moving in this direction.

Could one hope that the experiences gained in the Camphill communities would become seeds for the future, from which valuable contributions would spring towards the inevitably necessary changes in the development of society? Perhaps the continuous stream of earnest and bright, searching young people, who come to help in all the Camphill communities for varying periods of time, will be the wind to scatter such seeds.

——ACKNOWLEDGEMENTS——

The revised edition of 'Camphill Villages' has been made possible by the cooperation of members of Camphill communities – too numerous to mention – who supplied up-to-date descriptions of their places.

Photographs have also been provided of Rudolf Steiner by the Verlag am Goetheanum, of Karl König by Friedwart Bock, of Botton Village by Peter Mernagh, and of Botswana by Michael Peart.

Special mention should be made of Dave Layzell and Christopher Kidman for their editorial assistance and of Peter Mernagh and Andy Paton for their advice on photographs.

Contributions by the following to the 1977 edition have remained in this edition: Miss Gwen Gardiner, Antioch College, USA; Mrs Ursula Gleed, Counselling Service, Ringwood; Rev. Peter Roth, OBE, Botton Village; Dr. Thomas J. Weihs, Camphill Rudolf Steiner School Schools, Aberdeen. Thanks to Bill Shaw for his cover photograph, used in the first edition.

—FURTHER READING—

Chris Baum, Wain Farrants. *Camphill Address and Telephone Directory 1988*. Camphill Press, Whitby 1988.

Evelyn Capel. *The Christian Year*. Floris Books, Edinburgh 1982.

Evelyn Capel. *Seven Sacraments in The Christian Community*. Floris Books, Edinburgh 1981.

Michael Hailey, Vivian Griffiths, Boris Moscoff, Nicholas Poole. *Camphill Communities*. Association of Camphill Communities 1988.

Karl König. *The Camphill Movement*. Camphill Press, Whitby 1981.

Karl König. *A Christmas Story*. Camphill Press, Whitby 1984.

Karl König. *In Need of Special Understanding: Camphill Conferences on living with handicapped adults*. Camphill Press, Whitby 1986.

Rudi Lissau. *Rudolf Steiner Life, work, inner path and social initiatives*. Hawthorn Press, Stroud 1987.

Michael Luxford, ed. *Camphill Working Papers on Adolescence I*. Camphill Press, Whitby 1983.

Michael Luxford, ed. *Camphill Working Papers on Adolescence II*. Camphill Press, Whitby 1985.

Cornelius Pietzner, ed. *Village Life The Camphill Communities*. Neugebauer Press, Salzburg – Munich – London – Boston 1986.

Friedrich Rittelmeyer. *Rudolf Steiner Enters My Life*. Floris Books, Edinburgh 1963.

Rudolf Steiner. *Anthroposophy and the Social Question*. Mercury Press, Spring Valley, New York 1982.

Rudolf Steiner. *The Festivals and Their Meaning*. Rudolf Steiner Press, London 1955, 1981.

Rudolf Steiner. *The Social Future*. Anthroposophic Press, Hudson, New York 1973.

Rudolf Steiner. *Towards Social Renewal. Basic Issues of the Social Question*. Rudolf Steiner Press, London 1977.

Anke Weihs. *Fragments from the Story of Camphill*. Elidyr Press, Llangadog, Wales.

Thomas Weihs. *Children in Need of Special Care*. Souvenir Press, London 1977.

—ADDRESSES—

Camphill Village Trust Communities in Great Britain

Botton Village, Danby, Whitby, North Yorkshire YO21 2NJ, England.

The Counselling Service, The Studio, Ashley, Ringwood, Hampshire BH24 2EE, England.

The Croft Community, Highfield Road, Old Malton, North Yorkshire YO17 0EY, England.

Delrow College & Rehabilitation Centre, Hilfield Lane, Aldenham, Watford, Hertfordshire WD2 8DJ, England.

Grange Oaklands, Newnham-on-Severn, Gloucestershire GL14 1HJ, England.

Larchfield Community, Stokesley Road, Hemlington, Middlesbrough, Cleveland TS8 9DY, England.

Camphill Houses, 32 Heath Street, Stourbridge, West Midlands DY8 1SB, England.

Loch Arthur Village Community, Beeswing, Dumfries DG2 9JQ, Scotland.

Newton Dee Community, Bieldside, Aberdeen AB1 9DX, Scotland.

Other Camphill Communities in England, Scotland and Wales

Beannachar, Banchory Devenick, Aberdeen AB1 5YL, Scotland.

Camphill Blair Drummond, By Stirling, Perthshire FK9 4UT, Scotland.

Cherry Orchards Camphill Community, Canford Lane, Westbury-on-Trym, Bristol BS9 3PF, England.

Coleg Elidyr, Rhandirmwyn, Nr. Llandovery, Dyfed SA20 0NL, Wales.

Corbenic College, Drumour Lodge, Trochry, Dunkeld, Perthshire PH8 0BY, Scotland.

Craigmyle Community, Tornaveen, Torphins, Banchory, Kincardineshire AB3 4PD, Scotland.

Camphill Devon Community, Hapstead Village, Buckfastleigh, Devon TQ11 0JN, England.

Camphill Community East Anglia, Thornage Hall, Thornage, Holt, Norfolk NR25 7QH, England.

The Hatch, 23 Castle Street, Thornbury, Bristol, Avon BS12 1HG, England.

Camphill Milton Keynes Community, 7 Sterling Close, Penhyland, Milton Keynes, Buckinghamshire MK15 8AN, England.

Mount School Community, The Mount, Wadhurst, E. Sussex TN5 6PT, England.

Ochil Tower (Rudolf Steiner) School, Auchterarder, Perthshire PH3 1AD, Scotland.

Pennine Camphill Community, Boyne Hill House, Chapelthorpe, Wakefield, W. Yorkshire WF4 3JH, England.

Camphill Rudolf Steiner Schools, Murtle, Bieldside, Aberdeen AB1 9EP, Scotland.

Sheiling Farms Community, Folly Farm Lane, Ashley, Ringwood, Hampshire BH24 2NN, England.

Sheiling School & College, Horton Road, Ashley, Ringwood, Hants. BH24 2EB, England.

The Sheiling School, Thornbury Park, Park Road, Thornbury, Bristol BS12 1HP, England.

Simeon Care for the Elderly, Cairnlee Estate, Bieldside, Aberdeen AB1 9BN, Scotland.

Templehill Community, Glenfarquhar Lodge, Auchinblae, Laurencekirk, Kincardineshire AB3 1UJ, Scotland.

Tigh A' Chomainn Camphill, Woodlands, 4 Craigton Crescent, Peterculter, Aberdeen AB1 0FB

William Morris Camphill Community, William Morris House, Eastington, Stonehouse, Gloucestershire GL10 3SH, England.

Camphill Communities in Ireland

Camphill Community Ballytobin, Callan, Co. Kilkenny, Irish Republic.

Clanabogan Village Community, 15 Drudgeon Road, Clanabogan, Omagh, Co. Tyrone BT78 1TJ, N. Ireland.

Camphill Village Community Duffcarig, Duffcarrig, Gorey, Co. Wexford, Irish Republic.

Camphill Community Dunshane, Dunshane House, Brannockstown, Near Naas, Co. Kildare, Irish Republic.

Glencraig Community, Craigavad, Holywood, Co. Down BT18 0DB, N. Ireland.

Mourne Grange Village Community, Newry Road, Kilkeel, Co. Down BT34 4EX. N. Ireland.

Grangemockler Camphill Community, Temple Michael, Grangemockler, Carrick-on-Suir, Co. Tipperary, Irish Republic.

Camphill Communities in Central Europe

Village Aigues-Vertes, CH 1233 Chèvres-Bernex, Genève, Switzerland.

Fondation Perceval, Route de Lussy, CH 1162 St-Prex, Switzerland.

Humanus Haus, Beitenwil, CH 3076 Worb 2, Switzerland.

Foyer de Vie: Le Béal, F 26770 Taulignan, France.

Heimsonderschule Brachenreuthe, D 7770 Überlingen, West Germany.

Heimsonderschule Bruckfelden, Adalbert Stifter Weg 3, D 7771 Frickingen, West Germany.

Heimsonderschule Föhrenbühl, D 7799 Heiligenberg-Steigen, West Germany.

Camphill Dorfgemeinschaft Hermannsberg, D 7799 Heiligenberg-Hattenweiler, West Germany.

Camphill Dorfgemeinschaft Hausenhof, Altheim 59, D 8531 Dietersheim, West Germany.

Camphill Dorfgemeinschaft EV, Lehenhof, D 7774 Deggenhausertal 2, West Germany.

Karl-König-Schule Nürnberg, Zerzabelshofer Hauptstr. 3-7, D 8500 Nürnberg 30, West Germany.

Thomas-Haus Berlin, Peter-Lenné-Str. 42, D 1000 Berlin 33 (Dahlem).

Camphill Liebenfels, Sozialtherapeutische Werk und Wohnstätten, A 9556 Liebenfels – Kärnten, Austria.

Stichting Christophorus, Duinweg 35, 3735 LC Bosch en Duin, Netherlands.

Het Maartenhuis, Ruyslaan 81, 1796 AZ De Koog (Texel), Netherlands.

Camphill Communities in Scandinavia

Vidaråsen Landsby, N 3240 Andebu, Norway.

Hogganvik Landsby, N 4210 Vikedal, Norway.

Solborg-Alm, N 3520 Jevnaker, Norway.

Jøssåsen Landsby, N 7550 Hommelvik, Norway.

Vallersund Gård, N 7167 Vallersund, Norway.

Sylvia-Koti, SF 16999 Lahti, Finland.

Tapolan Kyläyhteisö, SF 16350 Niinikoski, Finland.

Staffansgården/Mickelsgården, Furugatan 1, S 82060 Delsbo, Sweden.

Camphill Communities in North & South America

Camphill Soltane, Nantmeal Road, R.D. 1, Box 300A, Glenmoore, Pa. 19343, United States of America.

Camphill Special Schools, Beaver Run, R.D. 1, Glenmoore, Pa. 19343, United States of America.

Camphill Village USA, Inc., Copake, New York 12516, United States of America.

Camphill Village Kimberton Hills, P.O. Box 155, Kimberton, Pennsylvania 19442, United States of America.

Triform, R.D. 4, Box 151, Water St., Hudson, New York 12534, United States of America.

Camphill Village Minnesota, Rt. 3, Box 249, Sauk Centre, MN. 56378, United States of America.

Camphill Village Ontario, Inc., RR 1, Angus, Ont., Canada L0M 1B0.

Angaià Camphill do Brasil, Caixa Postal 1122, 36100 — Juiz de Fora — MG, Brazil.

Camphill Communities in Africa

Camphill Community Rankoromane, P.O. Box 34, Otse, Botswana.

Camphill Village (Alpha), Kalbaskraal, 7302 Western Cape, Republic of South Africa.

Camphill Farm Community, P.O. Box 301, Hermanus, 7200 Cape Province, Republic of South Africa.

Camphill School, P.O. Box 68, Hermanus, 7200 Cape Province, Republic of South Africa.

Cresset Camphill Community, P.O. Box 74, Halfway House, 1685 Transvaal, Republic of South Africa.

Novalis House, P.O. Box 267, Halfway House, 1685 Transvaal, Republic of South Africa.

For telephone numbers of individual houses and workshops in the different Camphill communities, see the current 'Camphill Address and Telephone Directory', which is revised about every three years.

Cover photograph : Botton Village, Danby Dale.